THE NO-NONSENSE
GUIDE TO DIVORCE

THE NO-NONSENSE GUIDE TO DIVORCE

Getting Through and Starting Over

LORI HELLIS, JD

ROWMAN & LITTLEFIELD
Lanham • Boulder • New York • London

Published by Rowman & Littlefield
An imprint of The Rowman & Littlefield Publishing Group, Inc.
4501 Forbes Boulevard, Suite 200, Lanham, Maryland 20706
www.rowman.com

86-90 Paul Street, London EC2A 4NE, United Kingdom

British Library Cataloguing in Publication Information Available

Library of Congress Cataloging-in-Publication Data

Names: Hellis, Lori, 1956- author.
Title: The no-nonsense guide to divorce : getting through and starting over
 / Lori Hellis.
Description: Lanham : Rowman & Littlefield, [2022] | Includes
 bibliographical references and index.
Identifiers: LCCN 2021045529 (print) | LCCN 2021045530 (ebook) | ISBN
 9781538155592 (paperback) | ISBN 9781538155608 (epub)
Subjects: LCSH: Divorce—United States. | Divorce—Law and
 legislation--United States.
Classification: LCC HQ834 .H45 2021 (print) | LCC HQ834 (ebook) |
 DDC 306.890973—dc23
LC record available at https://lccn.loc.gov/2021045529
LC ebook record available at https://lccn.loc.gov/2021045530

♾™ The paper used in this publication meets the minimum requirements of
American National Standard for Information Sciences—Permanence of Paper
for Printed Library Materials, ANSI/NISO Z39.48-1992.

CONTENTS

ACKNOWLEDGMENTS

No book ever gets written without the support of many people and my heart is full that I have so many people to thank. Any expression of gratitude must begin with thanking every client I've ever represented for entrusting me with the most important matters in their lives during a most difficult time. I've learned something important from each of you, and your trust has meant the world to me. I also want to thank all the generous colleagues and friends who helped and mentored me over the years. Despite everything people say about us lawyers, you give our profession great nobility.

Simple thanks do not feel adequate for my husband, Carl; my daughter, Kjersten; and my mom, Annie, for their steadfast love and belief in me. Thanks to my friend, Asa Aramburo, and my soul sister and former legal assistant, Marilyn Anibal, for their early reading; their perspectives and feedback were invaluable. Thanks to my friend and former MFA professor, Beth Alvarado, for her encouragement and support. Thanks also to Tucker Stosic for his help with graphics and Ricky Esquivias for being my website master.

Finally, I extend a huge thanks to my agent, Max Sinsheimer of Sinsheimer Literary; my editor, Suzanne Staszak-Silva; and my publisher, Rowman & Littlefield, for taking a chance on this book.

INTRODUCTION

I blame this book on the measles—and my parents' divorce, of course. When I was about eight, I had a nasty case of measles and spent weeks bedridden as a result. While convalescing, I ate lunch propped on the living room couch, watching reruns of *Perry Mason*. I loved the mad Perry skills that could make a bad guy (or occasional bad gal) stand up in a crowded courtroom and yell, "I did it!" I wanted to be just like Perry. These days, most children receive a vaccination for measles, and I worry they may not have the same ready opportunity to discover their life's calling. Think of it: is that the real reason some parents are anti-vaxxers? Do they secretly figure if their kid is tough enough to survive the measles, she might be tough enough to be a divorce lawyer? A couple of years after the measles, my parents let me stay up late to watch a network airing of *To Kill a Mockingbird*. Honestly, I still suffer a lingering weakness for a man in a well-tailored linen suit (or man in uniform, but that's an altogether different story for a different book).

When my parents sadly and painfully divorced a few years later, I felt powerless. Much later, I realized that both adults and children feel powerless during divorce. Then, when my daughter was born, I felt just as powerless. I found I wanted to pour everything I knew from my head into hers so she wouldn't have to learn hard lessons by trial and error. Then I found myself wishing I could do the same for my clients.

So, dear reader, I've learned a few things in twenty-seven years of practice: tip your head, and I'll pour over some wisdom that could save you from the more painful or foolish (although sometimes funny) pitfalls. To quote my grandmother, "I hope you get a blessing from it." Except sometimes, she said it in French.

When I began this book, pandemics were in movies and Stephen King novels, and vaccines were for measles. Now, as I finish, COVID-19 is a sharp reality, and experts warn that the virus will have far-reaching future social and economic impacts. The pandemic as social experiment promises ripples in our pond that we will feel for generations. Lockdowns forced parents to assume more significant roles in childcare and education, and gender equality may have slipped into the background. Some families found themselves moving back to the traditional homemaker and breadwinner family model. Stressed parents juggled work calls and children's distance learning as families fought over bandwidth. The shift away from centralized offices may be a permanent change for many and means fewer people are tied to their geographic location, and families are on the move. Small spaces that functioned well for people who lived primarily outside their homes are now bursting at the seams. People in urban areas are migrating away from cities and into suburban and rural areas. New York, Chicago, and Los Angeles are all seeing outflows as modern-day pioneers move from cities to smaller towns like Jackson Hole, Wyoming; Bozeman, Montana; and Bend, Oregon— stretching small-town infrastructure to bursting. Housing prices in those newly desirable areas are inflating beyond anything we saw during the bubble of the early 2000s. Psychologists list the top stressors in life: marriage, divorce, moving, illness, job loss, and death of a loved one as some of the most difficult to navigate. The pandemic has dished a heaping helping of all of them, often all at once, and many marriages haven't survived the strain.

Economic divides are growing to chasms as our communities split into essential workers who must go to jobs and workers who can safely remain at home behind their computers. Now, as in past times of uncertainty, couples are postponing weddings, and dating may be difficult, if not impossible. Some young people have intentionally chosen to delay marriage and childbearing, and lowering birth rates will have a trickle-down economic consequence as fewer new workers replace aging baby boomers.

Those who are married may not stay that way. Many states are seeing increased divorce filings. Take a family where marital discontent has been at a low simmer, add job loss, the pressure of working while trying to educate children at home, too much togetherness, the loss of outside activities, the deaths of loved ones, and the overall sense of fear and hopelessness the pandemic has caused, and the simmer is now a full boil. There's never been a better time for a straight-talking book about the realities of divorce. So, as the punchline to a very old joke goes: hold on to your hat—we may end up miles from here.

DISCLAIMER

This book is intended to give general advice. It is not intended to replace consultation with a qualified attorney in the reader's jurisdiction. No universal laws govern domestic relations; all family law is state law. For that reason, it is essential to consult with an experienced local attorney if you are facing a divorce.

I've represented hundreds of clients in family, criminal, and juvenile cases over the years, and I learned something from every one of them. The illustrations I use here are fictional composites drawn from every one of those cases. There are common themes in endings and new beginnings. To protect and honor my clients' privacy, I have drawn anecdotes and illustrations from those themes and not from any specific case.

Part I

IT'S STARTING

What is marriage? I suspect you're thinking, "If I knew that, I wouldn't need this book." Stay with me, though, because to understand this book, it's important to know what the law thinks marriage is.

From a legal standpoint, marriage is a bundle of rights that two people get when they formalize a romantic relationship and make it a legal partnership. Those rights are important. Married people can inherit from one another, make medical decisions for each other, own property together, file taxes jointly, incur debt together, and share assets like retirement accounts and government benefits such as Social Security. When you divorce, you are essentially unbundling and disentangling some, but not all, of those rights.

When we flushed the British out of the United States with the Revolutionary War, they left their legal system behind like a ring in the bathtub. The American legal system is derived from English common law. Throughout the centuries, both English and American common law became codified in legal statutes. Our U.S. Constitution identifies the things that are the responsibility of the federal government to regulate. The Fourteenth Amendment gives the states the right to govern citizens in every other matter not explicitly assigned to the federal government. In reality, that's most things, including defining and regulating marriage and divorce.

Our American legal system is based on rules. We call those rules laws or statutes, and they govern individual behavior for the greater good of society. Laws govern behavior to keep us safe and our society orderly.

1

There are rules we lawyers call "black-letter law." Those are rules lawyers consider carved in stone. This book contains my own set of black-letter rules, and the following chapters explain how "**The Rules**" apply to your divorce.

THE RULES

Rule 1: *Whatever this shit is, it belongs to you. Don't make your shit your children's shit. Ever.*

Rule 2: *Keep yourself and your kids safe from the shit.*

Rule 3: *Never confront a person who is irrational, intoxicated, or both.*

Rule 4: *Don't lie. Not to your lawyer, not to a judge, and not in court documents.*

Rule 5: *Kids before cash.*

Rule 6: *Don't hide income, property, or debt.*

Rule 7: *You're impaired. Don't do stupid shit you'll regret later.*

Rule 8: *Don't blindside your ex-spouse.*

Not all marriages end in a volatile blaze; some end with a whimper or a sigh, but every divorce begins in a stew of pain and mistrust. Maybe it's because the person you trusted with your heart is not who you thought they were, or perhaps you are not the person you thought you were. Either way, radical change is ahead.

All self-help books cast a wide net. Not everything in this book will help every reader, but I hope everything in this book helps someone. Don't be surprised if important information gets repeated. I have found that people benefit from repetition, especially in the stressful early days of their divorce. You could be tempted to skip chapters you think may not apply to you, but please don't. There is essential information in each one.

It may feel like I've directed this book at highly contested divorces because I have. Your divorce doesn't have to be hostile and nasty, but aiming this information at the worst-case scenario gives you a chance to weigh choices, avoid pitfalls, and choose a best case instead. In truth, most couples never see the inside of the courthouse; most reach agreement on all the issues in their divorce before a trial is ever scheduled.

They either work out the details together, or their lawyers negotiate a resolution, or they use the services of a mediator. See chapter 18 for a complete discussion of mediation.

Over my long career, I have represented men and women nearly equally. While some things may be unique to each gender, most of my advice is universal, and I've tried to use *he* and *she* and the more grammatically challenging *they* interchangeably. Writers struggle with the dynamic evolution of language, and there's nothing more charged than the language around gender identity. Historically, marriage was a legal construct entered into by people of opposite sexes. Since 2015, our concept and understanding of marriage have been expanding. To quote the sign that is to be found eternally, in every airport, "Please excuse our dust; we're expanding." I've tried to do my best to capture and respect the appropriate pronouns, but understand that we may have evolved even further by the time you read this. Most of the book's advice applies equally to any divorcing couple; chapter 12 addresses specific concerns unique to same-sex couples. I recognize and care that not all families are made up of mommies and daddies, and you may need to insert your own titles or pronouns mentally. Our language around these concepts is still cumbersome and challenging for both writers and readers, but this is your book. Feel free to change pronouns and titles like Mommy and Daddy with the stroke of your pen if needed to make them feel applicable to your situation.

The days and weeks at the beginning of divorce are some of the most unsteady and uncertain you will experience. People facing divorce may do things that they would never otherwise consider. In most cases, cooler heads will prevail in time, but expect the unexpected and strive for everyone's safety until that happens.

1

THE BEGINNING OF THE END

No matter how it starts, the end of your marriage brings physical and emotional upheaval. The winds of change are beginning to feel like a hurricane. You can take comfort knowing you are not the only one experiencing this storm and that you will get through it.

SOMETIMES THEY LEAVE

Your spouse will never say they want a divorce when you've just had a shower, finally achieved washboard abs, or just had a pedicure. They will tell you when you are changing the car's oil or the baby has diarrhea. It rarely happens when either of you has just landed a big promotion (unless, of course, your spouse has just made partner and also tells you that they just need to see where this "thing" with Chad is going). In other words, you are not going to feel good about yourself. In fact, you are going to feel pretty shitty about yourself for a while. Sometimes you and your spouse have "the talk," and sometimes, a process server or a deputy knocks on your door. Either way, for the rest of your life, you will remember the sound of the knock, the door slamming, or the car backing out of the driveway. You even might think you won't survive the pain. You will.

Here is my advice for that moment: take a shower. And while you're in there, have a good, long cry. From now on, consider your shower your wailing wall; lather, rinse, and repeat as needed. Oh, and since no one ever felt better about themselves while wearing dirty sweats, put on clean underwear and some clothes that you would not be embarrassed to be seen in at the grocery store. Hose off the baby after his most recent bout of diarrhea and call your mom. If you can't call your mom, call someone you wish was your mom, and talk to them until they tell you they need to go to the bathroom or take their medicine. Be advised that if you talk so long that you hear the toilet flush, the next time you need to talk to the person you wish was your mom, they may not take your call.

Put the baby to bed, speed-read *Goodnight Moon* to your three-year-old, and tell your teenager to get off their phone. Pour the beverage of your choice and go electronically stalk your spouse. We both know you're going to, but be warned: you are going to find things you can't unsee. You will inevitably find the odd, friend-of-a-friend connection that leads to the fake Facebook account they use for Tinder, or the hidden overdraft notices, charges on a credit card you never thought to look at, or bank accounts you didn't know existed. In this interconnected world, even Bill Gates couldn't cover his tracks, and let's face it, your ex (get used to calling them that) is no Bill Gates.

Now would be an excellent time to head back to the shower. Keep breathing, and once you think you can't cry anymore, try to sleep. You might sleep, but you might not; either way, the sun will come up, the baby will need changing, and the teenager will have just gotten off their phone. Once the sun is up, feed all living creatures in your house, and don't forget the dog.

You may explain to your children that you are feeling sad. You may *not* tell your children, "Daddy/Mommy is a fucking asshole," even if he/she is. It's time for **Rule 1**. Think of it as the Prime Directive (It's a '60s TV reference—Google it): ***Whatever this shit is, it belongs to you. Don't make your shit your children's shit. Ever.*** Please note that I underlined, bolded, and italicized it because it's *that* important.

As soon as office hours allow, call your doctor. Hide in the bathroom for privacy if you need to; you'll get used to it. One of my clients called the bathroom her "Cone of Silence." (It's another '60s TV reference—Google it because if I have to explain every obscure cultural reference, we'll never get to the important stuff.) Get an appointment with your doctor as soon as you can, and while you have them on the phone, ask them for a referral to a therapist because you could be seriously losing your shit. For future reference, this is what temporary insanity looks like (next time, you'll be more generous when you spot it in your friends). Your emotions are on a roller coaster. They will go up and down without warning. Try not to resume destructive habits like smoking, drinking, or overeating, but don't be too hard on yourself if you already did. Using alcohol or drugs won't avoid the pain; it'll just delay it. There is an exception to the no drugs rule, of course, and that's taking prescribed antidepressants while engaging in some old-fashioned talk therapy. Medication and therapy won't help you avoid the pain, either, but they will help you process it faster, which is why I suggest you call your doctor and find a therapist right away. It's unlikely you will need long-term medication or therapy, but getting them on board now may make the next few weeks bearable. If you can't afford a therapist, call your local county behavioral health office and ask for an intake appointment.

If you are recovering from addiction, *disregard the advice above* about trying not to resume destructive habits and get to a twelve-step meeting *immediately.* Call your sponsor; call every name on your list, pack the kids in the car, and go. It doesn't matter if it's not a child care meeting; pack some Legos and a couple of extra diapers because the people at the meeting will understand. Drive sanely, but directly, to the nearest and soonest meeting, even if it's not your homegroup and you don't know a soul. If you sing in the car at the top of your lungs, you may not even hear the little voice in the back of your head telling you to swing by the liquor store on your way.

There will be things to do right away and things that can wait. The following few chapters will help you sort out which is which.

SOMETIMES YOU LEAVE

Sometimes you get to the frayed end of the day, walk through the door, and think, "I just can't do this anymore." You married a flawed human being. At some point, you loved them; perhaps you still do. But fifty or five hundred ways, there are as many reasons for going or staying as there are marriages. You may suspect you are imagining things when everyone around you thinks your spouse is perfect. Your parents love him; your friends think she's the best mother they've ever met. But no one lives in your marriage besides you and your spouse, and only the two of you are experiencing it from the inside. No matter why you are considering leaving, remember **Rule 1**: *Whatever this shit is, it belongs to you. Don't make your shit your children's shit. Ever.* There also may be reasons to stay, and sometimes it's hard to decide. This book isn't about deciding. That said, a client of mine, who was an engineer, told me he took out a piece of paper, divided it into two columns, then wrote "reasons to stay married" on one side and "reasons to get divorced" on the other. He assigned each entry a value between one and five. When he added up the columns, the score in the "get divorced" column was higher. He showed me this list the first time he came to see me. He'd scored his wife a three in the "stay married" column under "good mom" but scored her a five in the "get divorced" column under "spends too much." It turned out his wife had recently discovered the poker machines that the state lottery sponsored for "entertainment purposes only." She had been gambling every day on her lunch hour, and since the machines she liked were in the tavern near work, she was also drinking a few beers.

This book isn't about deciding, but you may have picked this book up, still wondering if divorce is the right choice for you. To paraphrase Paul Simon again, there may be fifty ways to leave your lover and just as many reasons not to. No one but you can know for sure if and when the time is right to divorce. I've had clients who agonized over the decision for months or years and clients who told me they just knew—like someone switched a light on. I've rarely had a client tell me it was an easy decision. Sometimes, if you are an analytical type, making a list of pros and cons can help. For others, simply forcing yourself to mediate quietly and sit with your feelings is enough.

I have a theory about pain. As you'll learn, I have theories about a lot of things. There are significant differences between how Western cultures approach pain and grief and how Eastern cultures do. For example, let's say you sustain a cut to your forearm, and you put a bandage on it. Every day, you look at the bandage and think, "I should take that bandage off." Every day the bandage gets a little dirtier. You know the bandage is no longer useful and may even be causing an infection. Still, if you pull off the bandage, it's probably stuck to the wound and certainly stuck to the hairs on your arm, and tearing it off is going to hurt. Here's the difference between our Eastern culture friends and us: we will avoid pulling off the bandage at all costs because we don't want *ever* to feel any pain. We'll avoid removing the bandage even when we know it's served its purpose and that for the wound to heal it needs to come off. Our Eastern friends look at pain differently. They understand that pain is temporary and that it eventually will pass no matter how bad it is. Right? After all, your knee isn't still hurting from that time you fell off your bike when you were eight, is it? We can learn a lesson from Eastern culture about coping with grief and pain: it's going to hurt, but sometimes, the best we can do is sit with the pain, accept it, let ourselves feel it, and wait for it to pass. It *will* pass even though it doesn't feel like it right now, and you will rise—healed and stronger.

Ending your marriage is hard, but truthfully, sometimes you just know. You come home from work, discover there's no bread, and realize it's the final straw, and as you pack a bag, your bewildered spouse asks if you're really leaving because there's no bread. All you can say is "yes." Yes, because you don't have the energy to explain. Yes, because it's going to take everything you have to let the door slam or back the car out of the driveway.

It hurts now, but you will heal; your children will heal. You know you're going to be okay because you are going to approach this change with thought, heart, and intention.

SOMETIMES THEY'RE ADDICTED OR MENTALLY ILL, OR BOTH

This section and chapter 3 deal with those emotionally charged relationships where one spouse suffers from addiction or domestic violence is a factor. Not all marriages involve these factors, but when they do, the need to act is urgent.

A psychologist would say addictions and mental health problems often "co-occur." In layman's terms, it means your spouse can be both addicted and mentally ill. You're thinking, "Yay! How did I get so lucky?" The short answer is, people with mental health problems self-medicate, and addiction makes people irrational. This leads me to **Rule 2**: *Keep yourself and your kids safe from the shit*. It won't be as simple as it sounds when your spouse is spiraling deeper into their illness.

Sometimes, you reach the bitter end when your spouse is drunk and angry again, or can't get out of bed again, or decides to rewire the house at 2 a.m. again, and you know you need to protect yourself and your kids from the shit. It isn't always easy to leave safely, and you may not be thinking clearly, so here's **Rule 3**: *Never confront a person who is irrational, intoxicated, or both.* Keeping yourself and your kids safe may require you to be patient and do some sneaky shit. You might have to leave for the grocery store wearing flip-flops and never go back, or you might have to pick the children up early from school and take them somewhere safe. When making a plan, assume your ex, who was not that smart when covering their tracks, either suddenly became brilliant or has hired a brilliant investigator and lawyer. Safety always comes first; see chapter 3 for specifics.

When addiction enters a marriage, it's as if the addicted spouse invites an unwanted guest who won't move out and uses all the toilet paper. Worse, no one consults the un-addicted spouse about inviting this guest. Even when your spouse's addiction isn't part of a more significant mental health problem, addiction causes extreme dysregulation to the emotional balance of a relationship. In English: addicts are selfish, irrational people, even if they aren't self-medicating a mental condition.

I like to use images to explain ideas, and here's the first of those images. Rube Goldberg was an engineer and political cartoonist who, in the 1920s and 1930s, drew funny, complicated machines designed to do a simple task. He used his cartoons to illustrate government waste, but the idea applies here. Imagine one of Goldberg's machines: a series of falling dominoes starts the sequence, the last domino hits a little car that rolls down a track, the car hits a spring that releases a boot that kicks a bowling ball that rolls down a ramp and squeezes toothpaste onto a toothbrush. After every squeeze of the toothpaste, somebody has to reset the complicated machine; in this case, that somebody is you.

The recovery community calls you an enabler or a codependent spouse. You convince yourself if you "just do this one thing" for your addicted spouse, life will be easier for both of you. In reality, your relationship is seriously out of balance; what actually happens is that the addicted spouse goes merrily on their way, abusing the substance of choice while the nonaddicted spouse builds and maintains an ever-increasingly complex life-support machine. The codependent spouse spends all their time lining up the dominos and resetting the spring-loaded car, all the while planning to expand the engine so it can also feed the cat. The metaphor applies no matter which substance your spouse abuses. Why does a codependent spouse go to such great lengths to enable an addicted spouse? Experts call it denial; regular people call it fucked up, and either way, we do it because we're afraid. Afraid of what might happen to our spouse, what the world might think, how the kids will cope, or what you'll use to pay the bills. And we wonder, "What's wrong with me?"

Nothing. Make no mistake; addicted people are selfish, and your spouse is more than happy to let you shoulder the shame and blame.

Healthy relationships are like a series of overlapping circles:

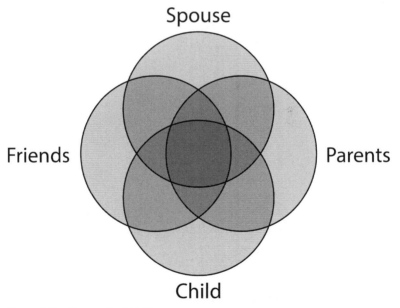

Figure 1.1. *Source*: Lori Hellis

But this is how your addicted spouse relates to the world:

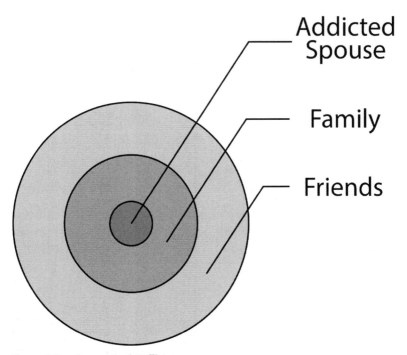

Addicted
Spouse

Family

Friends

Figure 1.2. *Source:* **Lori Hellis**

Yes, what you've always suspected is true; your addicted spouse does think they're the center of the damn universe. Furthermore (I had to throw in a *furthermore* to remind you I'm a lawyer), your spouse plays the victim whenever they can to keep the world orbiting around them and their addiction. Your spouse is happy—if the world thinks there is something wrong with you, it's not them. Recovery programs such as Alcoholics Anonymous, and other twelve-step groups, aim to move the addicted person from the target diagram to the overlapping relationship diagram by teaching the addict to ask how their actions affect the people they care about. Scientists tell us addicts' brains are hard-wired by addiction to avoid taking responsibility. I'm not a scientist, but I think it's because taking responsibility would require them to admit addiction makes them assholes. Well, it does.

I've had clients who find porn sites on their children's computers, clients who stumble across methamphetamine in the glove box or marijuana in the diaper bag, clients who find that their life savings have disappeared into the coin slot of a lottery machine, and countless clients who've received the 4 a.m. call from the drunk tank. Just when I think I've heard it all, I hear a new one; a recent client told me his spouse was secretly taking out federal student loans in his name and spending the money on her addiction.

Perhaps by the time you read this book, you'll already have tried to get your spouse the help they desperately need. My clients have often said it was important to them to feel like they had done everything they could before ending their marriages. Your spouse may be earnestly telling you they will get help. This marital crisis could indeed be the catalyst for your spouse to get help, and they might genuinely mean it; but remember, addiction is like a sneaky lover. While your spouse may want help, their addiction is also telling them that promising to get treatment is an excellent way to convince you to keep resetting the dominos and expanding their life-support machine. By all means, encourage your addicted spouse to get treatment for their addiction. But by no means allow their assurances to affect your decisions. Recovery from addiction is a long and fraught journey of fits and starts and relapses. It requires hard work and a lifelong commitment. When your spouse begins recovery, it's best in the early days to take the wait-and-see approach.

While things I've said in this chapter might seem eerily familiar, I have not been living under your bed with the dust bunnies and a single lost sock; they sound familiar because you're a codependent spouse. Codependent spouses are often also adult children of addicted parents, so let's be clear: you couldn't fix your addicted parent, and you can't fix your addicted spouse. The only thing you can fix is how you deal with the addicts in your life. Many support groups offer help for spouses and children of addicts, and I highly recommend them. The best-known organization is Al-Anon. If you log in to al-anon.org, you'll find helpful information and a meeting locator. While I think the in-person meetings are the most beneficial, many offer electronic options. You may think you are in this alone, but attend a single Al-Anon meeting, and you'll discover you are among friends.

Whether they leave, or you leave, whether your spouse is addicted, or you're just incompatible, you are at the beginning of a difficult period. No matter how our society values independence and self-reliance, you weren't meant to do this alone. Seek the help and support of friends, family, and professionals. Accepting help now means that you will be able to offer help to someone else later.

Be gentle with yourself, your spouse, and your children because adjusting to this new reality will require you to extend some grace to yourself and everyone else involved.

And don't forget to breathe.

2

SOCIAL MEDIA

Social media plays a role in nearly every phase of our lives, and just so you know, social media and divorce do not play well together. I have been in more than one trial where attorneys mined social media accounts for damaging information. Once that photo of you on the stripper pole surfaces, it will be hard to explain that it was taken at a bachelorette party ten years ago before you had kids. It's better if it's not there to find.

You may be one of the fortunate people whose divorce is friendly and who can discuss these issues with your spouse. Or you may be a person whose divorce starts out amicable but becomes more contested as time goes along. You may not need the social media precautions I outline here. I raise the issue out of an abundance of caution; once things are on the internet, they are difficult to get rid of.

At the beginning of your divorce, it may be hard to tell which way it will go, and it's better to be safe than sorry. I recommend that you scrub your social media accounts as clean as possible and set your privacy settings to the equivalent of "not nobody, not no how" (Google it, my pretty). You might overlook some of the more obscure things. Remember to check for memes or comments posted by someone else that you've "liked," blog posts you've written and posted, or posts you've "liked" on a blog platform like Medium or Tumblr. Don't forget to scrub posts on your Reddit, Discord, or LinkedIn accounts and delete the silly TikTok pandemic videos you've been doing about how much you drank during 2020. And it goes without saying, but still, I must: delete every dating profile and scrub your presence from every dating account on Earth. I don't care who you hook up with, but I guarantee your ex's lawyer will.

Be sure to tell your lawyer everything about your social media presence because deleting things doesn't protect you from the screenshots someone may have already grabbed. Once you have your public face scrubbed, stay off social media and do not post anything about your situation. I mean it. Don't post "FML, divorce sucks" or that cute picture of one of your children mixing you the cocktail you call "mommy juice."

If you operate a business that depends on a social media presence, keep your personal situation and your divorce out of it. That might be tricky if your business involves social media influencing, or you blog regularly about home and family. Unless you are highly monetized and rely on your followers for income, keep your divorce off your social media accounts. If you absolutely must blog or post about your divorce, be sure you are saying things you would be happy to have a judge or a child custody evaluator read. Something like, "even though our family is going through a hard time, I know we still care about one another and can be fair and make good choices that will be best for everyone." And don't worry if it's not true because no one is 100 percent truthful on their social media accounts anyway.

Once your divorce is final, odds are you are going to see things on your ex-spouse's social media account that you don't like. You're going to discover those photos of your child riding a bicycle without a helmet or hanging over the fence at the zoo trying to pet the tiger. You're going to find out your spouse has a new partner, took an expensive vacation, got a new car, or took up the hobby you always wanted to do together. Your ex will also undoubtedly catch that post of you at the lake doing shots around the campfire, or that time you posted the picture of the split lip your child got learning to water ski. You have two choices: keep watching and pretend you're not, or stop following your former spouse. Otherwise, you will both be revenge posting for years to come.

Mothers tend to be more risk averse when it comes to our children. Moms generally have no sense of humor when it comes to their children doing risky things. If you want to build trust with the mother of your children, keep the kids safe, and don't post stuff on social media that you know will make her angry or anxious, even if it is fun.

Some parents do not want their children on social media at all, and there are many reasons to keep your children out of view. If you happen to be someone in the public eye, keeping your child off social media may be a safety issue. Perhaps you're a lawyer who doesn't want your children targeted by a client's disgruntled ex—oh, wait, that was me. Some parents fear that putting their child on social media can invite sexual predators. Whatever the reason, the more restrictive choice should prevail, even if you think it's unreasonable. If you like sharing your children's activities with friends and family, consider a different, more private platform or determine if resetting your privacy settings will make the other parent more comfortable. Many of the coparenting sites I've listed in this book's resources section in appendix A include the option to create a page where you can share with friends and family.

Unloading your feelings by uploading is ill advised even after your divorce is final. Child custody and parenting time are always modifiable, meaning your former spouse can take you back to court if there is a change in circumstances. If you don't want your ex to use it, don't post it, and don't post it and then take it down because there's a good chance your ex or one of his friends will capture it in a screenshot.

While we're at it, let's remember that your children may also have a significant presence online. Have a frank discussion with your kids about the dangers and damage their social media posts could cause. Ask them not to comment publicly about your divorce and what your family is going through. These precautions might be tough with teenagers, and if your divorce is an amicable one, they may be unnecessary. As with all phases of your divorce, it's important to think things through and be intentional about your choices.

If necessary, explain that you want your child to have an outlet for their feelings but that it's vital that they not use social media for that purpose. I've seen cases where a child confides in a friend by text or on a "private" social media platform, only to find that when the child has a falling-out with the "friend," things the child thought were private become painfully public. Such a disclosure can make your divorce more difficult, but more important, it can embarrass your child. Make sure you explain that even platforms where posts "disappear" aren't safe because there are always ways to preserve those posts. Sit down with them and help them go through their privacy settings. I realize that it feels intrusive, but you can assure them that it's temporary.

3

RESTRAINING YOURSELF
OR OTHERS

While some marriages end amicably, some only end when one spouse escapes, like a caged bird, after weeks, months, or years of emotional, physical, or sexual violence. According to the National Coalition against Domestic Violence, one in four women and one in nine men will be the victim of severe abuse at the hand of an intimate partner in their lifetime.[1] You can find more information at ncadv.org.

Let that statistic sink in a moment; if you meet three girlfriends for lunch or play golf with eight other men, one of you has been or will be the victim of abuse.

If you have been the victim of physical, emotional, or sexual abuse at the hands of your partner, you must observe **Rule 2**: *Keep yourself and your kids safe from the shit*. It won't be easy. Like most domestic violence victims, you have learned that standing up to your abuser gets you hurt. Abusers come in all shapes, sizes, and genders, and abuse comes in many forms. If your partner controls all the money in your marriage, and you can't spend a penny without asking, that's abuse. If your partner monitors your calls and e-mails or puts a GPS tracker on your phone or car to keep track of where you go, it's abuse. If it makes you feel fearful and powerless, it's abuse. At their core, abusers are anxious people who keep their anxiety at bay by keeping all the variables in their lives under strict control. They will control people and circumstances by whatever means necessary to keep their own anxiety in check. Victims of abuse are not just hit, kicked, slammed against things, or forced to have sex; they're also publicly or privately demeaned, kept penniless, deprived of sleep, isolated from friends and family, convinced they are valueless, and made to feel helpless and hopeless. Abusers are most dangerous when they feel out of control.

The first and most important thing you can do if you are in an abusive relationship is make a plan. Your plan should answer these questions:

- How do I keep myself and my children safe?
- How do I keep myself financially secure in the immediate future?

Depending on the level of risk in your situation, your plan may be as simple as leaving while your spouse is at work or as complex as a well-executed covert military operation. The plan may involve only you, or it might involve trusted family and friends or community support such as churches, shelters, or other agencies that offer help. It's a good time for a Google search. If you are concerned about your partner finding evidence of your searches, consider using a friend's computer or one at your local library. When you make your plan, focus on **Rule 2**: *Keep yourself and the kids safe from the shit* and its companion, **Rule 3**: *Never confront a person who is irrational, intoxicated, or both.*

Your plan must include getting a restraining order and making arrangements for a safe, confidential place to stay for at least the first few days. In divorce, as in many parts of life, it is important to "begin as you mean to go on, and go on as you began," to quote Charles Spurgeon's well-known sermon, "All of Grace."[2] Tactically, that will mean making the first move to keep the upper hand. It's going to feel strange and frightening at first because your partner made you feel powerless, but you must push through the fear to safety.

In many states, marital assets, especially joint accounts, may be frozen, or your access to your money may be limited once you or your partner files for divorce, so it's essential to secure your share of the liquid assets before either of you files for divorce. While I never advise clients to take more than they are entitled to, I do advise clients to withdraw up to half of the money in joint accounts before they file for divorce. If you don't have a credit card that is only in your name, apply for one. These things will give you some breathing room and avoid the possibility of the other spouse using money to control you.

I also advise clients to keep their children with them in an undisclosed location, if necessary, until their spouse has been served with the restraining order and custody and parenting time has been established by court order. Remember, these are short-term plans for safety; if that means the children don't see the other parent for a few days, or the bills go unpaid for a month, so be it. Your safety is worth it. Overcoming the emotional toll abuse takes will not be easy. I'm sure it's not what you would expect me to say, but before you can escape or move on, you must cope with the shame. To be clear, you don't deserve the shame, but you will feel it; until you name it and come to terms with it, you will suffer. Once you understand that what you are feeling is shame, you can conquer it. Your partner will make you feel you deserve every bit of the physical or emotional abuse they're doling out. Your partner will convince you that if you were only smarter, or better at sex, or money management, or keeping house, or parenting, or providing, they wouldn't be forced to abuse you.

In case you missed it, that's some twisted shit. The brilliant Dr. Brené Brown has spent her career researching shame, and if you want to spend a life-changing twenty minutes, watch her TEDTalk, "The Power of Vulnerability."[3] Dr. Brown says that while guilt is a healthy emotion that helps keep us accountable, shame is corrosive. While guilt is about something you have done or left undone, shame is about who you are. Recognizing and acknowledging your misplaced shame is the first step to a healthier relationship with yourself and others.

If you are reading this and thinking, "my God, she's describing me! I'm a victim of abuse," tell someone you trust and get help now. Contact your local domestic violence agency; most counties have advocates who will put you in touch with resources and help you get a restraining order. Many counties have shelters and offer grants to help you pay the deposit on an apartment or rent a U-Haul.

Imagine I am sitting behind my fancy lawyer desk and using my sternest lawyer voice as I say "ask for help," because help rarely comes looking for you; you have to seek it out. Reaching out for help might mean calling the police if you feel unsafe. You may think that calling the police won't help and might make things worse, and yes, there are still places in the country where law enforcement officers treat domestic violence as a "family matter." Fortunately, that's happening less and less. Many states have a "must arrest" provision in their law that requires police to identify and arrest the aggressor in a domestic violence incident.

RESTRAINING ORDERS

It's time to apply for a restraining order. The laws and procedures about restraining orders differ from state to state, but fillable forms are generally available from the court clerk in person or online. Fill out the forms and be specific; most statutes require you to prove that a physical injury or a threat of physical injury happened in the recent past and reasonably caused you fear. If your abuser threatened to kill you and you believed them, that's probably enough. Provide dates and places, even if you can only remember the month and year. Submit the forms to the court (you would be surprised how many people fill them out but never turn them in). In most jurisdictions, a judge will hear the restraining order ex parte, which is a Latin phrase designed to make everyone think judges and lawyers are smarter than you. It means "one party" and signals that your abuser will not be there when you go before the judge to ask for the order.

The judge can order your spouse to leave the home and stay away from you and your children at home, work, and school. The judge will make temporary orders about custody and parenting time (some states still call it visitation); the judge can require that someone supervise the abuser's parenting time. Many jurisdictions have an agency that provides supervision for court-ordered parenting time. In most states, the judge can also order temporary child or spousal support. The Federal Violence against Women Act gives the judge in all states the right to limit the abuser's ability to own or possess firearms while a restraining order is in effect. States differ in the way the limitation is triggered and when and how it ends.

It's essential to follow the restraining order steps carefully. A judge must sign your restraining order, and the order must be served on your spouse before it becomes effective. In most jurisdictions, the sheriff serves restraining orders, and court personnel will advise you how to get your order to them for service.

Your spouse is entitled to ask for a hearing to contest the restraining order. In many states, the restrained spouse may also ask for a police officer to stand by briefly with them while they return to the home to gather immediate necessities like clothing, tools of their trade, and medicine. When your spouse asks for a hearing, they may contest either the underlying abuse allegations, the custody and parenting time provisions, or both. Not everyone asks for a hearing, but if your spouse does, the court must set a hearing within a short amount of time. In some states, the prohibition against possessing firearms is only triggered once there is a hearing, while in others, the ban stays in place unless and until there has been a hearing and the court orders otherwise. Courts are careful to protect everyone's safety while conducting restraining order hearings. Still, if you feel unsafe in the courtroom, tell the judge's clerk, and ask that a court security officer stand by in the courtroom. You may feel safer if an attorney or domestic violence advocate attends the hearing with you.

People have been known to misuse restraining orders to gain the upper hand in disputes over custody or support. Please don't be one of them. You should only obtain a restraining order if you are genuinely afraid for your safety. Gaming the system could delay the process for people who actually need restraining orders, could make your spouse less cooperative later, and will most certainly make you look like an asshole.

If your spouse serves you with a restraining order, comply with it to the letter. Do not make any attempt to contact your spouse. That includes contact through a third party. Do not respond to your spouse if they contact you. If your spouse is the one who asked for the order, they can't be found in violation of the restraining order, but you can. If you disagree with the order or want to change anything about it, you must ask a judge to change it. At a hearing, you can ask the judge for permission to contact your spouse through a third party or for the limited purpose of arranging parenting time or paying bills. If you go to court and the order is modified in any way, keep a copy of the modification with you at all times. Changes to orders don't always make it into the law enforcement database, and you might need to prove the changes if asked by police. If you violate the restraining order and your spouse reports it, the police must arrest you. If there is probable cause to believe you violated the order, police will charge you with a crime. If your spouse later drops the restraining order, the criminal charge still stands because the order was in effect at the time of the violation. In most states, violating a restraining order is a misdemeanor.

IT MIGHT BE YOU

If you read this and think, "I'm not abusive because I've never hit my spouse," you might be right. But if you have a history of calling your spouse fat, ugly, or a loser; accusing them of being incompetent; or calling them a whore, you've abused them. If you have ever awakened them in the middle of the night to continue an argument, isolated them from friends and family, tracked their movements, or used money to keep them under control, you've abused them. Worse, if you've said and done those things in front of your children, you have abused them, too. If you are reading this and thinking, "my God, that's me, I am a controlling, abusive spouse!" pat yourself on the back for being more self-aware than 90 percent of your peers, then go get help. Most people who abuse their spouses don't set out to hurt the person they love, but their anxiety and need for control lead to frustration, and then that frustration explodes into anger and violence. I repeat: *get help now* because abuse escalates. There are varying views as to why abuse gets worse, but I think it's because the abuser needs to exert more and more control to keep their anxiety at bay.

KIDS AND TRAUMA

People who abuse their spouses sometimes also abuse their children. Even if you've never put your hands on your children, the cycle of violence from generation to generation is real. Allowing your children to witness domestic violence between you and your spouse is abusive. Children who witness domestic violence have alarming rates of substance abuse, depression, and suicide; they are also more likely to abuse their own spouses and children when they become adults. Perhaps you learned the behavior because you were raised in an abusive household yourself. Scientists have even identified subtle changes to abuse victims' genetic structure, causing what they call "intergenerational trauma." If your parents abused you, you have a responsibility to take control and stop the cycle by seeking therapy and treatment through a Batterer's Intervention Program (BIP). Don't let the title fool you. Don't think, because you never hit your spouse or your child, that treatment isn't for you; emotional abuse is still abuse, and they treat that, too.

Here is an excellent place to explain my pickle jar theory of trauma. Imagine I take an empty pickle jar down to the river and scoop it full when the river is running high and fast. Mud, silt, and debris have mixed with the water because of the turbulence. If I put the jar on my kitchen windowsill, eventually, all that muck settles to the bottom. The pickle jar is like us; the turbulence of a traumatic event or a lifetime of chaos has stirred up our water. Eventually, when things calm enough, the muck sinks to the bottom, and we live for a time in the clear water. But what happens when something triggers our old trauma, or some new trauma occurs? What happens when something agitates our pickle jar? We begin to suffocate in the muck.

Although divorce is stressful, and stress makes people lash out, abusive behavior is not a natural byproduct of divorce. If you or your former spouse are struggling with controlling abusive behavior, you owe it to yourself and your children to seek therapy immediately. If your children have been victims of physical, emotional, or sexual abuse, it is your responsibility to get help for them and find ways to keep them safe. Your child may not understand they are the victims or know how to ask for help, but you know, and it's never too late or too soon to begin the family healing.

The only way to truly change the endless pickle jar cycle of agitation and settling is to carefully siphon the muck off the bottom of the jar through therapy. Many experienced trauma therapists use a treatment called Eye Movement Desensitization and Reprocessing (EMDR). Not all experts agree on how EMDR works, but it does, and it can be an effective way to reduce the muck in the bottom of the jar and lessen the agitation. The treatment involves doing bilateral movement while recalling a traumatic event. Sometimes therapists use eye movements; others may use alternating tones through headphones. The brain is like a file cabinet, and experts theorize that posttraumatic stress disorder (PTSD) happens when the brain files a traumatic experience in the wrong place. The memory gets filed in the part of the brain that experiences things that are happening now. Every time you access the memory, all the same physiological symptoms are triggered; you experience the same freezing panic, sweat, adrenaline, racing heart, shortness of breath, and fight or flight reaction as if the remembered traumatic event were happening at that moment. Worse, the brain keeps rewriting that memory in the wrong place every time it's triggered. EMDR appears to help the brain move the memory to the part of the brain where the past is stored. For an excellent explanation of the impact of trauma on the brain, watch Dr. Dan Siegel's YouTube video "Hand Model of the Brain."[4] His theory is also sometimes referred to as "Flip Your Lid."

The next few stressful weeks may trigger past trauma. While you're busy keeping everyone else safe from the shit, be sure to take care of yourself, too. If you start therapy now, it will not only help you deal with the past but also help you move forward with strength and determination. Therapy is a safe place where you can take off your armor and allow yourself to be vulnerable, and it may be the only place where it feels safe for a while.

4

TELLING THE CHILDREN

The moment you tell people you are getting divorced, they'll all have an opinion. My grandmother used to say, "opinions are like assholes, everyone's got one," except sometimes she said it in French. Some opinions count more than others, like the opinions of your children.

If, when you think about telling your children, you feel like you're standing on the edge of a minefield, you are. What follows are some helpful suggestions on how to discuss your divorce with your children. Ideally, you and your spouse will have this conversation with your children together; but you're probably thinking, "if things were ideal, I wouldn't need this fucking book." Well played, dear reader. If possible, tell the children together, but at a minimum, please observe **Rule 8: _Don't blindside your ex-spouse_**; inform them you'll be telling the children and when. This small step is the beginning of building mutual trust around coparenting. See chapter 8 for a complete discussion of the "Trust Gap."

How to explain your divorce to your children depends a lot on their age and emotional development. Explaining your divorce to a five-year-old is somewhat different from the conversation you might have with a fifteen-year-old, but don't think that it will be any easier for your children if they are teenagers. No matter your child's age, strive to keep things as calm and normal as possible. You're the adult; if you're afraid and bewildered, imagine how your child, whose brain is still under construction, must feel. Your children need to feel you have things under control, even if you know you don't. It's another one of those "fake it 'til you make it" moments adulthood always seems to be tossing us.

Any parent who has packed the peanut butter and grape jelly sandwich and strawberry yogurt in the same place in a Spider-Man lunchbox day after day can tell you children hate change. Changing routines, homes, and schedules will not be easy for your child. Don't make the mistake of going in depth when explaining your divorce to your children; they're not mini-adults. Resist saying "Mommy and Daddy don't love each other anymore," because it'll only make them wonder if you will stop loving them, too. Unlike adults, children live firmly in the now. Developmentally, they are self-absorbed creatures who can only think about how this new situation impacts them. Think of them as emotional radar detectors. They can't intellectualize what is happening to them; they just run around sucking emotion out of the air. Reassuring your child that their physical and emotional well-being is not in jeopardy staves off more complicated questions and makes them feel secure. Your children want answers, and the simpler and more straightforward, the better. The same advice applies to teenagers, but for slightly different reasons, as you'll see later in this chapter.

What will happen to me? Your answer should be gentle and reassuring. "Mommy and Daddy both love you, and we'll both work hard every day to make sure you are okay." Although it's tempting, please avoid things like, "You and I are going to end up living in the rat-infested gutter while your asshole daddy and his slutty secretary drink champagne in Paris," even if it is your worst fear.

Where will I live? Be honest but reassuring. If you know, give specifics. Children's physical surroundings are paramount to them, and they think in concrete ideas. They want to know how big or small the new home is, what color things are, even how it smells. If you don't know, you might say something like, "Mommy and Daddy are still figuring it out, but don't worry; you'll still have your favorite things." Please note, "I don't know because your money-hungry mother is going to make me sell your precious childhood home and give her half the money" is not the correct answer.

Where will Daddy/Mommy live? No, you may not answer, "In hell." There are some situations where one parent may be moving farther away. Be honest. There are questions you won't be able to answer right away, but tell them what you can, and to the extent possible, how it will impact them. If you don't know the answer yet, a simple "We don't know yet, but we're working out those details" will have to do. Don't be afraid to promise to tell them as soon as you know, but be sure to keep the promise.

Will I still see Mommy/Daddy? You may feel like answering, "over my dead body," but that isn't going to make your confused child feel any more secure. Some of this depends on the safety of the situation. Assuming there are no safety concerns about the other parent, the correct answer is, "It might be a little mixed up at first, while Mommy/Daddy and I figure it out, but you'll see both of us a lot." Allow me a quick aside here about the time parents spend with their children: God, nature, or the Big Bang who created us designed us to need our children. If we didn't, we'd go all *Mommy Dearest* on them when they discover they can reach the wallpaper from their cribs (yes, once again, Google it). As much as you need to put your nose behind their little ear and inhale to make the world feel less wobbly, they need that, too, and they need that from both parents. To be clear: you don't have visitation rights; your children do. Visitation is for their benefit, not yours. Your children need both their parents, so limiting their time with either of you without a damn good reason might make you feel better, but it's unfair and unhealthy for them.

Can I still have my same friends/hobbies/sports/school? I'm sure you know by now, saying, "Your friends' parents are all on Daddy's side and hate us, and we won't be able to afford athletic cups and cleats anyway" is not the correct answer.

I suggest a blanket statement like, "Mommy and Daddy are not going to live in the same house and be married anymore. Grownup stuff is complicated; it's why they pay us the big Mom and Dad bucks. It's not your job to figure things out; that's our job. Your job is to play and learn. We both love you a lot, and we'll always take care of you. Mommy/Daddy will live in this house, and Daddy/Mommy will live in another house. You'll live with Mommy/Daddy some days and Daddy/Mommy the other days. Sometimes it'll be hard for me not to be with you all the time, but it'll be a lot easier knowing you are with Mom/Dad, who'll take good care of you. (Yes, I do know you may have to say it through gritted teeth—but keep saying it until it's true.) You'll still go to your school, and you can still be friends with Jenny and Jacob.

Bosco, the family dog, will live at Mommy's/Daddy's. You can keep your favorite toys at whichever house you choose. Would you like a popsicle?" Giving children some agency, like where to keep which toys, and enough information to feel informed, makes children feel more secure. And popsicles help.

Children often act out their emotions because their brains have not developed enough to process complicated feelings. Most children adjust well, but I recommend seeking a professional's help if your child's behavior changes. If your child's grades fall, or if he loses interest in a favorite activity, experiences changes in eating habits, begins isolating, or engages in destructive or violent acts, seek immediate help from a licensed and experienced child therapist.

This is a good place to say a word about school: your child's teacher will appreciate it if you let them know your family is experiencing a divorce. The teacher will also appreciate it if you spare them the details and don't bad-mouth your spouse. Remember, teachers have to continue dealing with both of you, and you want the teacher to be fair to everyone.

Any parent with a child over twelve will tell you teenagers require special handling; think bomb-squad in a minefield precautions. For teenagers, the subject of their parents' divorce is fraught with questions about whether they had a role in causing the divorce, their own ability to form and maintain relationships, their sexuality, and their place in the family.

Teenagers often try to take charge. There are reasons for this; they might think their parents need protection, and they may also believe they bear some responsibility for the divorce and need to repair the situation. It's up to you to keep your teenager from becoming overly involved. Do not be fooled by their appearance; even though they shave, they are not adults, and you should not, under any circumstances, treat your teenagers as confidantes. They are not your girlfriends or guy pals, and ***whatever this shit is, it isn't theirs***. Your teenagers are still children, and they are experiencing one of the most terror-inducing events of their lives. While they may say they are relieved the fighting is over or that they understand the reasons, your children aren't really relieved, and they don't understand. They need to feel their parents are still in charge. Offer clear, straightforward explanations; don't be surprised if they push back; and don't forget the popsicle. When a horse trainer begins training a young horse, they start with the horse in a tiny enclosure where it feels safe. As the young horse gains more confidence, the trainer expands the size of the training ring. The same ideas apply to teenagers; proper boundaries help them feel safe.

Talking to your children about your divorce won't be one discussion but, instead, a series of conversations as questions arise and the situation evolves. Be clear about boundaries, and in all those conversations, resist the urge to let them make the decisions that are your responsibility.

Many people ask about the age at which children can decide. Some states allow children to make those decisions, but I don't recommend it. The fact that your fourteen-year-old wants to live with you now may feel good, but it doesn't mean it's the right choice for them. Advocating for more choice for your children because they prefer you can backfire when they decide they'd rather be with the other parent because there are fewer rules, a spare car, and the best PlayStation. Decisions about where your children live, their education, where they go, and when they go there are the responsibility of you and your coparent. Abdicating is never advised.

5

FINDING A LAWYER

L ook for a lawyer who doesn't just tell you what you want to hear but looks you in the eye and tells you the hard truth. Good lawyers explain the process and keep you apprised of developments, but they aren't your therapist. Choosing a lawyer requires deliberation, like choosing a counselor or a doctor or an expensive pair of shoes. Because doesn't it always come down to shoes? Or maybe that's just me.

How do you navigate the consumer nightmare of legal advertising to find the best fit for you? One of the best ways to find a lawyer is to ask friends and family, the same way you'd ask a friend where they got those comfortable-looking shoes. More than half of marriages end in divorce these days, so everyone knows a guy. Make appointments with several lawyers. While it's true that you get what you pay for, beyond a certain point, more expensive doesn't necessarily mean better. Find out what the average hourly rate is in your area. You can call your state bar association or check their website. Rates differ depending on your region of the country; fees are much different in Los Angeles than in, say, Laramie, Wyoming. Most attorneys charge for your initial consultation. An attorney offering free consultations is an attorney who is either new to the practice or hungry for clients for other reasons. The initial consultation tells you a lot about your possible match and if retaining that lawyer is worth your investment.

Is the lawyer interested in you and your problem, or are they just happy for someone to pay them to talk about themselves? That's something you'll want to know. It's essential that, when you look across the desk, you think, "there's someone in there who knows their shit, cares, and knows how to help me." If you don't get a good vibe in your first meeting, move on. I used to tell prospective clients, "I'm an acquired taste, and I'm not the right lawyer for everyone. If I'm not the lawyer for you, let's figure it out now, so we are both happy. If it's not me, I'll give you the names of the lawyers in town I would use if I needed a divorce." A bad fit is a waste of time and money for both you and the lawyer. In general, you want an attorney old enough to be experienced and young enough to have the energy for your case. Many ask, "Is it better to have a male or female lawyer?" And my favorite lawyer-ish answer is this: it depends. Sometimes women feel more comfortable with a woman, especially if there has been abuse or an imbalance of power in the marriage. I've also had male clients say they prefer a woman because they think a woman will be better able to stand up to their wife.

Large firms can be bureaucratic. Even if your initial consultation is with a named partner, they will likely pass your case off to a younger associate. Large firms sometimes churn files. The file might pass from associate to paralegal to assistant to file clerk, and every time someone new touches the file, you get billed. A smaller firm or single practitioner is less likely to do that.

Your lawyer's support staff can be more important to you than your lawyer. There is no doubt my long-time assistant was a huge part of my success; she was the glue that held everything together. While I was flying in and out of the office, off to hearings and meetings, she was fielding phone calls, scheduling appointments, collecting information, and generally helping my clients feel important and heard. Look for an attorney who takes a team approach and respects and honors their staff because the way they treat their staff is a good indication of how they'll treat you. Don't make the mistake of treating your attorney's support staff poorly. In my office, the quickest way to get shown the door was to mistreat my assistant. I could always get more clients, but a good assistant is hard to find.

Attorneys usually charge by the hour. In some kinds of cases, attorneys can represent a client on a contingency; that means they only get paid if you win, and they take a percentage of your winnings. Most states don't allow family lawyers to work on contingency. A few states permit it if the case involves collecting support or other divorce judgments once the divorce is final. Not permitting contingency fees makes sense; after all, how do you define winning? What if you get the house and your spouse gets all the cash? Do you owe the attorney one-third of your home? If you win custody, does your attorney get one-third of the children? Attorneys also charge what are called flat fees. In a flat-fee arrangement, you agree to pay the attorney a fixed amount of money, and they work on your case from start to finish, no matter how much time it takes. These arrangements can be deceptive, though, so be cautious. Flat-fee agreements usually say that the fee covers everything up to a trial, but if a trial is necessary, the client pays the attorney by the hour for trial and trial preparation. If you can't afford a retainer and your spouse can, your attorney may be able to ask a judge to order your spouse to pay your attorney's retainer. It's called suit money, and it's especially helpful in cases where one spouse controls all the family resources.

Lawyers sometimes offer flat-fee services for "uncontested" divorces. You may very well be fortunate enough to have an amicable divorce where you and your spouse have worked out all the details and just need help with the paperwork. Still, it's often hard to predict if your uncontested divorce will remain so or whether it might suddenly become hostile and hotly contested. Since flat-fee lawyers often withdraw or start charging a steep hourly premium if a case becomes contested, hiring such a lawyer can be costly.

You are not required to have a lawyer to get divorced. That said, going to court without one is terrifying and will probably disadvantage you. Modern alternatives to hiring a lawyer include online services, paralegals, document preparers, and lawyers who offer something called "unbundled legal services."

ALTERNATIVES TO HIRING A LAWYER

Let's look at the alternatives. If you are leaving a short-term marriage with minimal assets and debts, no real estate, and no children, any of the following alternatives could work. It's when your situation is complicated that the differences become problematic.

Document preparers do just what the title says. They draft legal documents. They can't give you legal advice or even tell you if you are filling out and filing the correct documents.

Similarly, paralegals prepare legal documents. They can't legally give you advice or appear with you in court. Sometimes they do give legal advice despite the rules, and their advice is often wrong. Yes, lawyers sometimes give bad advice, too. The difference is that lawyers are insured if they commit malpractice; document preparers and paralegals are not. When in doubt, hire a lawyer.

Many jurisdictions allow what are called "unbundled" legal services. That means you can hire a lawyer to do a single defined task, like draft a final judgment. Many lawyers and some clients find the arrangement problematic. Your lawyer can't represent both sides of a divorce. For example, if a couple reaches an agreement between themselves and one hires a lawyer to draft the final judgment, the lawyer they hire only has a duty to the person who hired him. Is the lawyer obligated to prepare the judgment as the couple agreed, even if it's a bad deal for the person they represent? What if the agreement is one-sided and unfair to the unrepresented spouse, or what if the represented spouse later decides they made a bad deal? You may think this is silly and that lawyers are just prone to angels-on-the-head-of-a-pin questions, but people are under a lot of stress during divorce, and in the heat of the moment, they can make agreements they later regret. When that happens, they invariably look for someone else to blame, and the lawyer is their likely target. Lawyers who offer unbundled services claim a well-written fee agreement can head off most of those problems. Other lawyers disagree. I've always felt if I advise a client from start to finish, I can be sure the client was getting the benefit of my experience and my considered opinion. If the client decided not to take my advice, at least I was sure they had all the information they needed to make a reasoned decision.

Here's the thing: lawyers are expensive. I can't tell you how many times someone told me they wished they made as much as I did in an hour. To be clear, your lawyer didn't put all that money in their pocket. They paid their office expenses, like rent, payroll, malpractice insurance, health insurance, and more. Your lawyer worked hard for four years to earn a bachelor's degree with grades good enough to get them into law school. Then, they attended three years of law school and studied for and passed a bar exam. When I graduated from law school in 1992, the average law student graduated with $60,000 of school debt. Today, that number has tripled. Once in practice, your lawyer keeps learning; they pay to attend continuing legal education classes and conferences and subscribe to court opinions and professional journals. They read books and articles about mental health and child development and attend seminars to improve their trial skills. They often volunteer both in the community or for the state bar association. Lawyers know their hourly rate sounds like a lot of money to the average person, and most lawyers want to be fair about their fees, but running a professional practice is expensive.

RETAINING YOUR LAWYER

Once you and your lawyer decide to work together, the lawyer will ask you to sign a contract with them. It might be called a fee agreement, a retainer agreement, or an employment agreement. You will find a sample retainer agreement in appendix B at the end of the book; yours may differ, depending on state laws. If you don't understand what the contract means, ask your lawyer to explain it in plain English. The contract spells out the services the attorney performs, what is expected of you, how much the lawyer charges, the minimum retainer, and the conditions under which each of you can terminate the agreement. The contract should say you can fire the attorney at any time and that the attorney will stop work if you don't pay them or disagree with their advice about your case's direction. Realistically the latter rarely happens because you are in charge of directing your case. If you decide you don't want half the interest in the house or you don't want spousal support, those decisions are up to you. I always reserved the right to withdraw from a case if I thought my client wasn't acting in their children's best interest. Not every lawyer sees it this way, so it's essential to discuss before you decide to retain someone.

Your lawyer will ask you to pay them a retainer. A retainer is a fund of money to ensure your lawyer's fees are paid. The money is held in a client trust account until the attorney earns it. It remains your money until it's earned. The lawyer keeps track of the time they spend on your case and withdraws their earned fees from the retainer every month. Your attorney should present you with a detailed monthly bill so you can keep track. If the case ends and there is money left over (it does happen), it should be refunded to you without any additional fees. If, as more often happens, there is casework left over when the retainer is depleted, you'll be required to replenish the trust account.

Most lawyers allow you to carry a small balance forward into the next month but may withdraw from your case if the balance isn't paid immediately. Likewise, most lawyers won't begin preparing for your trial unless there are sufficient funds deposited in your trust account to cover both the preparation and the trial. Preparing for trial can take from as few as eight hours to as many as forty or fifty hours. Expect your attorney to ask the court to postpone your trial and allow their withdrawal from your case if your trust account is empty. Your lawyer should be clear in their fee agreement about how you'll be billed. Talk to your lawyer openly and honestly about any concerns you may have about their billing practices. Most lawyers don't do their own billing and may not know something is wrong. We want happy clients, and we can't fix things if we don't know about them.

Expect to be billed when you call, text, or e-mail your lawyer, even if the lawyer tells you they have no new information for you. Lawyers charge in tenths of an hour and usually bill a minimum of two-tenths (.2). When your lawyer is talking to you, they can't be doing other work for other clients. Just like your plumber has to charge you for a service call even if there wasn't actually a problem, your lawyer has to charge even when there's nothing new to report. I always tell clients that while we are available if they need us, and I'm happy to talk to them, to keep the bill in mind when they are calling. I've learned some clients need more reassurance than others. If you want your lawyer to hold your hand, need someone to vent to, or just want her to act as your counselor and confidante, understand that it comes at a price.

As a rule, a standard letter takes about a half hour (.5); a long letter detailing a settlement offer might take as long as two hours. Drafting a motion or preparing a judgment takes about one or two hours. You can save yourself a lot of money by paying attention and being organized. At some point, your attorney will ask you for documents and information. You know your financial information and personal files better than anyone, and you can easily arrange them, tab them, and make extra copies. If the idea of facing that task seems so impossible that you throw it all in a cardboard box and deliver it to your attorney, expect to be charged for a few hours of staff time to sort, organize, and copy the materials.

If your lawyer needs experts, like an accountant, an appraiser, a psychologist, or a private investigator, you should expect to make financial arrangements directly with the expert. You should not expect your lawyer to advance those costs. We'll talk more about experts in chapter 19. Mistakes happen. Paperwork goes missing, return calls get overlooked, and typos sneak in. Ideally, your lawyer and her staff should catch them, bring them to your attention, and fix them promptly. Poor judgment and ignorance of the law are not mistakes. Not filing or serving documents properly, missing court appearances, or not meeting deadlines are not mistakes. They are the hallmark of an attorney who is not doing their best work for you. Keeping a law practice operating smoothly and juggling the professional and personal isn't always easy, and your lawyer might be in a difficult season. Don't be afraid to express your concern to your lawyer and expect a frank reply.

Sometimes, a prospective client would ask for a consultation with me to talk about leaving the attorney they've already hired. Those who think lawyers are only in it for the money may be surprised to learn I usually discouraged people from leaving one of my colleagues. Sometimes you feel you need to change lawyers because it's just not a good fit, but understand the change may be expensive and can be gut wrenching. Before you decide to dump your attorney, take time for a bit of soul-searching: is it them, or is it you? People getting divorced are fragile, frightened, irrational animals—imagine a deer in the headlights carrying a shotgun while wearing noise-canceling headphones. Before you jump ship, you might want to examine your expectations and review your lawyer's advice. Sometimes, conversations with your lawyer overwhelm you, and you shut them out. You may need to have your lawyer repeat their advice while you take notes or ask them to put their advice in a letter so you can go back and reread and process their advice.

Divorce laws are designed to deal with stuff, not emotions. If you're mad at your lawyer because she just doesn't understand your attachment to the red antique stove you lovingly refurbished, changing lawyers isn't going to help. If, on the other hand, you find you have retained an attorney who makes you feel insignificant or whose business model involves charging for passing the file through every hand in the firm, you might be better off cutting your losses and starting over. Ultimately, only you can decide.

Your lawyer should be a communicator with skin as thick as a rhino. Remember, they're used to getting their head handed to them by cranky judges and arguing points of law that would make anyone else's eyes glaze over. If you have a problem, talk to your lawyer—in person if possible. Make a list beforehand of all the things you are concerned about; if you're nervous, read her your list. Have your lawyer explain how they plan to respond to your concerns and how you can help. Set deadlines and make a mutual to-do list that you both understand and agree to follow.

Every state regulates lawyers and requires them to comply with a code of ethics. Why? Because lawyers have access to your most personal information and are responsible for advising you on some of the most important decisions of your life when you may be at your most vulnerable. If you are interested in reviewing your lawyer's ethical regulations, they are available on your state bar association's website. If, on the other hand, you'd rather be dunked in siracha than read the lawyer ethics rules, here's a rundown of the highlights.

To paraphrase the Bible, your lawyer can't serve two masters. The rule against conflicts is the heart of most ethics rules. An attorney can't represent you if they have previously represented or consulted with your spouse unless you give them written permission to do so. An attorney is obligated to keep everything you tell them confidential unless the information is life threatening. If you tell your lawyer you've picked up a particularly virulent and uncomfortable sexually transmitted disease that you intend to happily pass to your spouse, your lawyer can't disclose it. If, on the other hand, you admit to your lawyer that you just stopped by your spouse's office to cut the brake lines on his car, your lawyer is obligated to notify the police.

Likewise, if you happen to mention that someone is abusing a child or an older adult, your lawyer is required to call the police and child or senior protective services. Lawyers, like doctors, teachers, and counselors, are mandatory abuse reporters. Lawyers can't loan you money or go into business with you, and in most states, it's illegal for a lawyer to have a sexual relationship with you. These rules are in place to keep unscrupulous attorneys from taking advantage of vulnerable clients. While it should go without saying, I do have to say it: whether it's against the rules or not, if you sleep with your lawyer, you'll probably both get screwed.

6

FILING FOR DIVORCE
OR LEGAL SEPARATION

The next step will depend on your situation and the state in which you live. In some cases, couples reach an agreement to divorce and agree on who will file. In more volatile cases, the filing and serving of the documents can be tricky. If you are concerned with your safety or simply want to avoid a confrontation, a bit of planning will help. Your lawyer will prepare the documents, have you sign them, and file them with the court. Divorce documents commonly include the following:

- A Summons
- A Petition for Dissolution and any other supporting documents required by the court in your state
- Some combination of motions for Temporary Custody of Children or for Temporary Parenting Time, and Status Quo orders for custody or property, all with their supporting affidavits
- Motions for Temporary Exclusive Use of the family home and your vehicle and their supporting affidavits
- Motions for Temporary Child and Spousal Support and their supporting affidavits

Your divorce petition will follow a typical format. Most petitions allege general things. I've provided two sample petitions in appendix B, but yours could look very different. In some states, it's a form where you check boxes. As you can see from the samples, the petition is very general, addressing categories and not specifics. It's typical because lawsuits begin with general allegations and end in specific judgments.

Historically, a person seeking divorce had to allege grounds, but about half the U.S. states have passed some form of no-fault law. That means that neither spouse must allege grounds to justify their divorce; it's enough to say that the marriage relationship has irretrievably broken or that there are irreconcilable differences. In the states that still permit filings that allege grounds, the party filing the divorce may choose to file either using no-fault grounds or on the traditional grounds such as adultery, cruelty, violence, or abandonment. If proven, the grounds for the divorce can open the door to a punitive award of property or support in those states.

Every state requires that you establish yourself as a resident of the state before you can file for divorce there. Residency is what gives the court the jurisdiction and the authority to decide your case. The amount of time necessary to establish residency varies by state, and jurisdiction can be complicated.

If you already filed for temporary custody of your child in another state (perhaps through a restraining order), you still must meet the requirements of the Uniform Child-Custody Jurisdiction and Enforcement Act (UCCJEA) in the state in which you file. See chapter 20 for a complete discussion of the UCCJEA.

There is no real tactical advantage to filing first unless child custody is at issue and the filing spouse is seeking temporary custody in a no-fault state. As the filing spouse, if you intend to allege fault or ask for custody of children, you should file first. While it's not fatal to your case if your spouse files first, it may cause additional hearings over your temporary custody orders.

In most states, filing for divorce automatically triggers a temporary restraining order or injunction that freezes all your marital assets for everything but ordinary, day-to-day expenses. That keeps either spouse from cleaning out bank accounts, selling property, or otherwise disposing of or dissipating assets unless both spouses agree or the judge allows it. Most states also prohibit the cancellation of health insurance, auto insurance, and cell phone service without the agreement of both spouses or the court's permission. If your state does not have a law that automatically triggers an injunction, your lawyer should file a motion asking the court to issue one. The injunction acts to keep things stable until cooler heads prevail. Your lawyer will also advise you about other actions to take before you file.

If your spouse controls all the money, you might be wondering how you can afford to retain an attorney to file your divorce. Most states permit you to ask a judge to order that your spouse give you "suit money." That's money to retain an attorney and pay filing fees. Usually, your attorney will file your petition for divorce along with your motion for suit money. Once you have filed, you can also ask the judge for temporary child and spousal support and temporary custody. See chapter 7 for more information on temporary orders.

Once you sign your initial documents, your lawyer has filed them with the court, and a judge has signed any temporary motions, the documents must be served to your spouse. In most jurisdictions, you have the choice of having a uniformed law enforcement officer or a civilian process server deliver the documents. You may have a friend or family member serve the documents, but you may not serve them yourself because you are a party to the lawsuit for divorce. There are instances where having a uniformed officer serve your documents might be safer and instances where an officer at the door could inflame an already volatile situation. You are the best judge of which method is appropriate.

In most states, you may file for something called a legal separation rather than a divorce. A separation can do everything a divorce can do, such as determine custody and parenting time and divide property and debt, but it does not dissolve the legal marriage. In a narrow subset of cases, a legal separation may be appropriate. In those cases, perhaps the parties have a religious objection to divorce, or there are marital benefits, such as health insurance, that one partner needs and can't get outside the marriage.

Some people might see separation as an interim step or a way to wake up their partner. In those cases, legal separations most often become expensive divorces. Using separation as a step toward divorce often simply means doing everything twice.

7

NEXT STEPS

TEMPORARY SURVIVAL

The reality of what is happening has now set in; the first of the month is looming, and you are trying to figure out how to support two households. Decisions are coming at you fast and furious. My grandmother used to say (in French, of course), "You can eat an entire elephant if you just do it one bite at a time." As with any problem, it's best to take your divorce one step at a time, and prioritize oncoming challenges, so you deal with the most pressing ones first. Think of it as triage. When soldiers on a battlefield need medical attention, the doctors decide which cases are life threatening and deal with those first; hangnails go to the back of the line.

Divorce can be demoralizing, and the very human urge to keep things that embarrass us private is natural. Fight that urge and tell your lawyer, your landlord, and your creditors what is going on. Being honest about your situation may win you some grace. It also helps if you can show them you have a plan.

Shelter, food, transportation to work, and medical needs top the list, but this outline is only a starting point because every situation is different.

Shelter

Where will you live, how will you pay for it, who will live with you, and when? If you noticed that resolving this question overlaps with many others, you are not wrong. Answering this question will often mean conquering some of the other issues, such as support and custody.

Ideally, if you and your spouse have school-aged children, and it's possible, you should choose residences within the same school boundaries. Making that decision early in the process assures that the children will not have to change schools, and both parents will have access to the children's teachers and activities. It's not uncommon for divorcing people to move more than once during the first year or two as the situation settles, and it's also not always possible to keep the children in their same school.

Money

Before you can decide where you will live, you need to determine how much you can pay toward rent/house payments. That means sitting down and making a realistic and attainable budget. Two households cannot operate as cheaply as one, and each spouse will have to make some sacrifices. The first step is to wrangle all your expenses into a budget. If you and your ex-spouse are amicable, you can do it together. If not, start with your part. I have included a worksheet in the sample documents to help you think through all the present and future expenses (see appendix B). It is similar to the worksheet you will be required to file with any motions for temporary support. You should complete the worksheet using numbers that reflect your post-divorce living situation. Once you know your expenses, look for places where your expenses overlap with your former spouses or where you might economize.

Suit Money

If you are in a situation where you need your former spouse's financial assistance to retain an attorney and run up against their resistance, you will need to ask a judge to order your ex-spouse to help. People sometimes equate money with love and withhold money as punishment or to exert control. If you are thinking that way, and withholding money from your spouse, be aware that judges don't see it that way. In the current climate of no-fault divorce, the judge will not care if she had an affair or that he is emotionally abusive. A judge is merely going to look at the numbers and try their best to be fair. It's my hope that you and your spouse will approach your divorce with the same sense of fairness, but I know it's hard, especially in these early days.

Employment

If you have a job, you should keep it, but I understand divorce doesn't always wait for a convenient time. Many divorces happen in the middle of a career change, a financial crisis, or a medical emergency when situational stress brings the slow burn to an explosion. If you're contemplating a career change, it's probably best to wait until you finalize the details of your divorce. If you have been out of the workforce staying at home with children, this is an excellent time to assess your qualifications and research opportunities to refresh outdated skills or retrain for a different career. There has never been a time when distance learning was as easy as it is now. The changes to work norms thanks to the COVID-19 pandemic may also make it possible for you to start a new job from home. Yes, balancing children while working from home is challenging, but it is possible.

For many couples, there is a disparity in the spouse's employment status. One spouse might be at home raising the children or may be employed at a lower rate of pay. It can be frustrating to see your former spouse unemployed while you are working hard to support two households, and yes, it's especially galling if the unemployed spouse is the one who initiated the divorce. You might even wonder if you can force your spouse back to work. The short answer is no. Although your spouse may be more than qualified and more than capable of work, this isn't the time to insist on that point, especially if there are children involved. There will be time later to argue earning capacity and potential income when negotiating the final judgment or presenting your case to a judge.

Custody and Parenting Time

We will look in depth at these subjects in chapter 9, but for the moment, you'll need a general idea of how much time your children will spend with you and how much with your former spouse because child support is calculated based on how much time the children spend with each parent. Many states base support on the number of nights the child spends at each of your homes.

TEMPORARY CHILD AND SPOUSAL SUPPORT

Divorces take time. Even a straightforward and simple divorce can take months to finalize. In the meantime, you're going to need to take some temporary measures to keep things going. You and your spouse may be amicable and in complete agreement, but it's still a good idea to have written temporary orders signed by a judge. Friendly partners can become hostile under some circumstances, and sometimes, you can even disagree about your agreement. Did you agree that you would pay the house payment and spousal support, or did you understand that you would pay the house payment instead of spousal support? A written court order protects both of you from misunderstandings and the danger that the other person might change their mind.

There are other significant reasons why getting it in writing is vital. One reason is that judges often give weight to what you are already doing when they decide on permanent support. A court order that memorializes your temporary support may also be necessary for future tax purposes and will be needed to prove your income if you have a college student using your income to apply for financial aid.

Not all temporary orders automatically create enforceable money judgments. A money judgment is a court order, but not all court orders are money judgments that can be enforced by a garnishment or by the court holding the adjudged person in contempt of court. Contempt of court carries the penalty of fines or even jail time. Judges don't like having their orders violated. If it takes a year to finalize your divorce, you want an enforceable judgment in place that requires your former spouse to keep up on their financial obligations to you.

A judge can order temporary child and spousal support and determine who has possession and temporary use of the family home and vehicles. A judge can also enter what is called a "Status Quo" order. The term *status quo* means "as it is." Think of a Status Quo order as a snapshot of the present situation. A Status Quo order assures that the current situation stays the same until a judge signs your final divorce judgment.

A typical financial Status Quo order prohibits either party from hiding or liquidating marital assets and requires that neither person cancels the other's cell phone; or stops life, auto, or health insurance payments; or stops contributing to retirement accounts. All of these things are negotiable. For instance, a Status Quo order would usually keep you from selling your automobile. But if, for example, you and your spouse agree that it's necessary to trade your luxury car in for something more affordable, you could complete the transaction. If your spouse objects to trading in your car, you may still ask a judge to order it. And yes, sometimes passive-aggressive soon-to-be ex-spouses (one client called hers the "wasband") object to things merely to annoy each other or make life harder and more expensive. See chapter 8 for a complete discussion of the "Trust Gap" and why you should take the high road in these situations.

Even if there isn't a court order, don't cancel your spouse's car, home, or health insurance, and don't take them off your phone plan or drop them off your Netflix subscription. You may want to but don't. It's a shitty thing to do, and although it might make you feel good for a moment, it will undoubtedly create hard feelings that could plague your relationship with your ex for years to come.

Status Quo orders are not appropriate when you ask the court to change something you are already doing or order actions for the first time. In that case, you would have your lawyer file motions that ask the judge to decide those new issues. A temporary or Status Quo order may also determine temporary child custody and parenting time.

TEMPORARY CUSTODY OF CHILDREN AND PETS

Children are not property, but pets are. Weird, right? For those of us who consider pets members of the family, it seems odd. For those who think their children are extensions of themselves, it probably feels pretty odd, too. We will talk in depth about custody and parenting time in chapter 9. Here, we are just talking about what happens with children and pets between your separation and when your divorce judgment is final.

The law requires judges to keep the upheaval for children at a minimum. That's why most judges will enter a Status Quo order. The order will prohibit either parent from hiding or secreting the children, or changing their usual residence, schedule, or their parenting time with either parent. Think of a Status Quo order as freezing the present situation, like freezing the frame while watching a movie. Status Quo orders are designed to put things on hold until cooler heads—yours or the judge's—prevail. A temporary custody and parenting plan is just that—temporary. You are trying to give your children some certainty and stability in a situation that's moving faster than Quicksilver or the Flash. The way you negotiate this agreement will also set the tone for how you plan to go on in this new coparenting relationship. While it's true that temporary custody is often a starting place when judges decide the schedule, fear that you are setting a precedent should not be your first or even your second consideration. The well-being of your children should be your first concern.

This period of post-separation uncertainty comes at the worst possible time. You are reeling. You are angry, hurt, and disoriented from all the change, and now you have to be civil and thoughtful? Sorry, but yes. Even worse, things are going to change rapidly, and you and your spouse are going to have to adjust to new schedules and new responsibilities. It's going to require that you each give one another some grace. And, yes, I understand it's a tall order at this moment, but do it for your kids.

The question of where the pets will live is often as tricky as where the children will live. If the pet has been designated a service animal or an emotional support animal for someone in the family, it should remain with that person. It's essential to put the pet's interests first. If the pet is your children's best friend, it should stay with them. The pet should live where it will have the best life, regardless of your attachment. That means it should not be locked in your apartment for eight hours a day while you're at work if it can be happy living in the house with the big yard with your spouse.

I've had cases where people struggled to choose where a pet would live, and I've also had instances where partners used the animals to hurt or manipulate the other spouse. Like children, pets deserve a safe home where they are cared for.

Part II

THE ENDLESS MIDDLE

The middle of your divorce is the most excruciating. It will drag on and feel like it will last forever. It won't, but that will be hard to believe when you're feeling mired in the middle. Now would be a great time to distract yourself a bit. I mean with a new hobby, not with swiping right or left. Establish some new traditions or new goals, both individually and with your children.

8

THE TRUST GAP

Trust is that elusive state of safety, of having faith in another person, and of believing they will put your best interests before their own and remain loyal because they love you.

People don't get divorced because they trust each other; they get divorced in a stew of broken trust. In even the most amicable of divorces, both partners feel some level of betrayal. When we think about broken trust, we usually assume one partner has had a relationship outside the marriage; but trust breakdowns come in many forms, and things like broken financial trust can be every bit as damaging.

Once broken, trust is difficult to recover, but your relationship can't simply end when you have children. Instead, your relationship with your spouse has to undergo a radical change because finding a way to trust your former spouse is essential if you're going to coparent. You may never trust your former spouse with your heart again, but now you have to trust each other with the most precious thing in your life: your kids. It won't be easy, but for the sake of your children, you must reach the point where you trust each other to be good parents. You get there when you both commit to being unfailingly reliable when it comes to your children. You build that trust when you keep your word, are transparent about where the children are and what they do, don't pry into each other's business, and don't ask to change the schedule unless absolutely necessary (when you are sick or have to work, for example, not when your favorite team is playing or when you'd rather spend the afternoon with your new boyfriend).

Trusting parents communicate. Many former couples find it hard to talk on the phone, especially in the early days, and if that's the case, use text messages or e-mails. Texts and e-mails are a good idea for two reasons: first, you can compose, then edit your communication to make sure the message is thoughtful and neutral, and second, you have a written record of both sides of the conversation. If your child has a soccer game or an ear infection, let the other parent know. Many modern parents use Google calendar or one of several apps to help keep schedules straight. See the resources in appendix A at the end of this book for suggestions. Many apps even send you reminders when it's your turn to pick up the children. This one can be critical if you forget early release day or tend to get wrapped up in work and lose track of time as I do. Some apps also function as a social media platform where your former spouse or selected family members can post and view pictures or read a blog account of your time with the kids. It's also a handy way to let your former spouse know what you did while the children were with you and alert him or her to any issues, such as a child who is getting sick or an unfinished homework assignment.

We humans are hard-wired to need our children. If we weren't, there would be many more children left in highway rest areas. Divorcing parents often come to me, demanding their "rights" to see their children or seeking to limit the other parent's "rights." The law doesn't see it that way, and neither do most judges. Parenting time is for the benefit of your children, and it's their right, not yours. Your children have the right to spend time with both parents if they can do so safely. If you want to build trust with both your former spouse and your child, acknowledge that your child's time with the other parent is just as sacred as the time they spend with you.

To build that elusive trust, never change the schedule or make an appointment for the child, enroll your child in an activity, or RSVP for a party on the other parent's time unless your former spouse agrees. Welcome the other parent to attend activities, games, programs, and practices during your time. If there are practices, performances, or games that occur on the other parent's time, ask both the other parent and your child if they are comfortable with you being there, and respect their wishes. Successful coparents discuss their children's activities and decide together which ones will be best for the child while maximizing the time the child spends with each parent. Be on time. Ensure the child arrives at the other parent's home bathed, fed, and with all the things they need— even if your coparent doesn't return the favor. Pack the medicine, the favorite stuffy, or the ballet shoes. Your child needs to feel comfortable and safe. We are talking about your child here, not a bargaining chip to be used to inconvenience your former spouse. Try this strategy with your coparent: *ask for help*. When is the last time someone asked you for help and you said no? We're socially programmed to help someone who asks. Next time you want your ex to do something, instead of telling them to do it, tell them you need their help with something. You will be surprised what happens. Instead of demanding, you've enlisted your ex's help, and the two of you are working as a team and not at cross purposes. An argument over homework can turn from this: "Johnny didn't get his homework done again! Every time I send him to you, you never make sure he gets his homework done. Now he's failing math, and it's your fault!" To this: "Hey, I really need your help with something. Johnny's teacher says he's not doing well in math because he's not getting his homework done. It sucks that the teacher assigns weekend homework that has to be turned in on Monday, especially because he's always busy on Saturday with sports and then tired after the games. I'm thinking of making Sunday morning homework time so he gets it done while he's still fresh. What do you think? Could that work at your house, too?" It will not be easy. Do it anyway.

Return the children's clothes, clean if possible. Don't keep the child's things at your house without the other parent's agreement. Make sure your child does homework, school projects, and music practice while with you. Share sports equipment willingly. If you exchange the children at the end of the school day and your child doesn't like to telegraph that he or she is going between parents by hauling a suitcase, consider delivering your child's belongings to the other parent's home or office. Do not, under any circumstances, adopt a pet for the child and then insist the pet accompany the child to parenting time with the other parent. If you believe your child needs a service animal or an emotional support animal, discuss it thoroughly with your former spouse and your child's medical or mental health provider. Do not appear at your children's events with your new partner without giving your coparent and your child advanced warning and determining clear boundaries. No matter how wonderful you think your new love interest is, showing up with that person is like expecting your former spouse to run a marathon on a broken leg. When you are trying to rebuild trust with your former spouse and your children, showing up at your son's football game with your new partner will not help. Your former spouse, who already feels betrayed, is going to panic. For more on introducing a new partner to your children, see chapter 21.

Treating your former spouse with respect and consideration may be the most challenging but important thing you'll do. Do it because it will pay huge dividends in the future; a few concessions now could make high school graduations and weddings in the future not just survivable but enjoyable. It doesn't mean you won't have to use your shower wailing wall or lock yourself in your car alone while you scream at the top of your lungs about what an asshole your former spouse is. Feel free. But most important, remember **Rule 1**: *Whatever this shit is, it belongs to you. Don't make your shit your children's shit. Ever.*

9

CUSTODY AND PARENTING TIME

No subject is more fraught with pain, anxiety, and anger than child custody, and when you are facing divorce, it's the thing you don't want to get wrong. Adults often recall with sadness and disgust their own parents wrangling over custody and parenting time. Your divorce may trigger memories of sorrow from your own childhood experiences. Now, you're feeling broken and are hurting, and you're still expected to make the right choices for your kids. Sorting out all those feelings is yet another reason therapy might be helpful now. The way you approach parenting your own children during your divorce is crucial. The decisions you make for them about custody and parenting time should be made thoughtfully and intentionally. Many states require divorcing parents to attend an education seminar on parenting strategies during and after divorce.

Think about what your spouse holds most dear. I hope it's your children, and you should, too. If it's not, the decisions now around custody and parenting time may be much easier, but I think your children's future lives will be much harder. As I've mentioned before, we humans are biologically programmed to need our children, so deciding to spend less time with our children means fighting our own internal wiring. It doesn't feel good. If you assume your soon-to-be ex is struggling with those same emotions, your discussions about custody and parenting time can be more empathetic, productive, and respectful.

Now is a good time to tell you my theory about the tennis shoe and Tahiti. When I was a young adult, Michael Jordan was at the pinnacle of his basketball career, and Nike was churning out Air Jordan shoes as fast as their factories could produce them. Air Jordan basketball shoes, which had a cushion of air sealed in each sole, were manufactured in China and

57

shipped to the United States on colossal container ships. One of those ships sailed into a terrible storm, and a full shipping container of Air Jordans washed overboard. The waves broke the container open, and the air in the soles caused the shoes to float. The accident set a fleet of Air Jordans sailing the Pacific Ocean. Thanks to the prevailing wind and seas, the shoes began washing up along the Oregon coast. Beachcombers found them left and right, and small beach towns began having monthly match parties, where you could trade shoes to make pairs.

Contrast this with another story, where I reconnected through social media with some people I went to high school with. One guy had spent thirty years building a sailboat in his backyard. Through the ups and downs of his life, he remained dedicated to building this boat. He moved it with him when he moved houses and slowly and methodically assembled it piece by piece. When he retired, he posted pictures of himself and his wife on a beach in Tahiti, frosty rum drinks in hand, and his sailboat at anchor in the distance. You might think the two stories are unrelated, but here's the connection: you can live your life like a tennis shoe, floating wherever the wind and waves blow you, or you can build a sturdy boat and chart a careful course. Either alternative is acceptable, but if you choose to live as a tennis shoe, you can't bitch when you end up on the cold, rainy Oregon coast rather than in sunny Tahiti. You might argue that most people are a bit of both or that the best-laid plans can go awry, and you'd be right on both counts. But the chances of actually getting where you want increase exponentially when you actually chart a course and lay in supplies for the trip. The time to be a tennis shoe is not when you make decisions about your children's custody.

CUSTODY IS ABOUT DECISION MAKING

Custody is a legal concept. It dates back to when a man's wife and children were considered his property. (Just in case you missed this significant historical development: spouses are no longer personal property and neither are children.) States are moving away from the concept of custody entirely, but even in those states, the legislature recognizes that someone has to be the children's shot caller. Some states presume that both parents are fit and that parents should have equal custody unless the court orders otherwise. Other states refuse to mandate coparenting unless both parents agree. In all jurisdictions, custody is about which parent will make the major decisions for the child. Those major decisions include whether the children will attend public or private school, their religious education and training, and nonemergency medical treatment (which could include body piercing and tattooing).

I know of a case where a couple fought for years over who would decide their child's elective surgery. The dispute arose after the father converted to Judaism and wanted his son circumcised. They fought in court for most of the son's adolescence, filing appeals until the case reached the state supreme court. The case went on so long the question finally became irrelevant when the boy turned 18 while the case was still on appeal and could make his own choice.

While sole legal custody means one parent makes the major decisions, joint legal custody means the parties confer about those major decisions. Clients often ask, "What happens if we can't agree?" The answer is that a judge may have to decide for you. That judge might also decide joint legal custody isn't working for you and order that one or the other of you have sole legal custody.

If your spouse adopted your child, or you are the adoptive parent of a stepchild, the law treats that child as if they were born naturally to you and your spouse. The adoptive parent has the same responsibilities and the same custody rights as any natural parent. Most states have a process that permits a stepparent to adopt their spouse's child legally. The process generally requires that either the child's biological parents both consent to the adoption or that the birth parent and the adopting parent prove the child has been abandoned by the parent whose parental rights they seek to terminate. This book isn't about stepparent adoption. If you are interested in a stepparent adoption, you should consult a family lawyer in your state. Most states allow for a stepparent to step into the shoes of a biological parent legally, but few states allow a birth parent to voluntarily terminate their parental rights outright. States want children to have adults who are physically and financially responsible for them.

Throughout the years, I've had clients come to me, demanding that I defend their "parental rights." I quickly disabuse them of any notion that they have rights that are somehow superior to the other parent. Let's have a quick refresher on the U.S. Constitution. The Constitution restricts what the government can do to curtail individual rights. In most cases, the Constitution says the individual's rights take priority over the government's. In a few instances, for the greater good, the Constitution grants power to the government that is superior to the individual to maintain good order and protect everyone's rights equally.

You and your spouse each have certain constitutional rights as a parent. You have the right to make decisions about your children's health, welfare, and education without interference from the government. Like all constitutional liberties, this one is not unlimited. In most states, some form of education is compulsory. Likewise, you may not physically or sexually abuse your children; withhold food, water, or medical care from them; or offer them for sale (no matter how they may tempt you). In short, parenthood comes with substantially more responsibilities than rights. You're not constitutionally guaranteed custody or parenting time. Custody is decided based on what is in your children's best interest. If you and your former spouse can't decide what's best for your children, a judge will. Parenting time is for the benefit of children. Let me repeat that for emphasis: *Parenting time is for the benefit of children.* The law presumes that it's in your children's best interest for them to have a close, loving relationship with both their parents. Still, if a judge determines it's not, custody and parenting time can be restricted or denied.

Clients also come to me demanding to know if their children have rights. Often, this is because they want their children to have the right to refuse to see the other parent. Your children do have rights. They have the right to be safe, healthy, protected, loved, and educated, and those rights trump parental rights. In some states, when children reach a certain age, they can choose which parent they want to live with. In my experience, allowing young teens to choose puts too much pressure on an emotionally fragile, developing young psyche. It's unusual for a young teen to be able to intellectualize the choice. Rarely have I met a teen who tells me, "I want to go live with my dad because he makes me do my homework, insists I have a curfew, and limits my screen time." More often, the choice favors either the parent who the child thinks needs them the most or the parent with the fewest rules, a spare car, the fastest Wi-Fi, and the best gaming system.

PARENTING TIME IS ABOUT
SPENDING TIME WITH YOUR CHILDREN

For most parents, the issue of legal custody is less important than the practicality of how much time the child will spend with each parent. When I began my practice, there was a groundswell from father's rights groups to mandate equal time for each parent. While the importance of children spending time with both parents can't be overemphasized, psychologists quickly pointed out problems with the 50-50 scheme.

We were thinking like lawyers, ready to split the baby, but the experts pointed out that children thrive best on consistency. Schlepping children back and forth between two homes frequently guarantees both parents get to see their kids' faces, but it gives the kids a case of emotional whiplash. On the other hand, neither parent wants to be the one who takes their kids bowling on Sunday and calls it good. Striking a balance requires thought, cooperation, and a careful gauge of your children's individual needs. Some children are unfazed by rapid and frequent transitions, while others find any amount of change unsettling; most kids fall somewhere in between. The ideal schedule should allow both parents to interact with their child's school, teachers, activity leaders, and coaches and give each parent the chance to develop routines around bedtime and homework.

Over the years, I've consulted with many child psychologists. Most of them said children should go to sleep in the same bed as often as possible, meaning that they should have one primary home. Psychologists warn that children learn to form attachments and come to believe the world is a place they can trust, based on how predictable their lives and relationships are. The younger the child, the more critical consistency is.

Some parents have responded to their children's need for consistency by adopting a scheme experts call "nesting-in." Nesting-in is an arrangement where the children remain in the family home, and the parents switch who lives in the house with the kids. It's a scheme that has faded in popularity as a long-term parenting-time plan. There are advantages and disadvantages to the arrangement. The advantage is that the children remain in their familiar surroundings, which may give them a sense of continuity. Parents often use it as a temporary arrangement to lessen tension while working out a more permanent plan. There are disadvantages as well. Neither the parents nor the children can make the mental shift from intact family to divorced. Instead, nesting-in exists in a sort of an emotional gray area that keeps the couple enmeshed with each other. Nesting-in may work in the short term, but as parents pull away and begin to establish their own lives and identities outside the marital relationship, it will become more complex. Nesting-in also requires a level of communication, cooperation, and coordination that challenges most divorcing couples.

One parenting-time scheme that is successful for younger children is a 5-4-9 plan. The numbers refer to the number of overnights the child spends with each parent. Under the plan, Parent A has the children Sunday evening until Thursday evening in week one (five nights), then Parent B takes over. The children are with Parent B from Thursday evening until Parent B drops them at school on Monday morning (four nights). Parent A then has the following nine nights until Thursday evening of the next week. This schedule allows the child to maximize a home routine while Parent B still has meaningful time. Ideally, Parent B also sees the children sometime during Parent A's extended nine-night week, usually for dinner. If the exchange happens at school, be prepared to drop your child's suitcase and sports equipment off at the other parent's home or work; kids don't like taking a suitcase to school. We'll cover how to share holidays later in this chapter.

Very young children have little concept of time, which makes it difficult for them to get into a time-sharing routine. They are creatures of the moment. Their ability to think about the past, present, and future in a linear way doesn't begin to develop until sometime in middle school. When my daughter was in sixth grade, her math teacher required that she turn in weekly homework on Wednesdays. Every Sunday, I would remind her of her math homework, and every Sunday, she would tell me she had time because it wasn't due until Wednesday. I would then have to remind her that she had choir practice on Monday and sports practice on Tuesday, and then I would ask her when she thought she would have time to complete the work. It took many weeks before she finally understood that she would need to plan her work, although Wednesday seemed far away. This same child didn't master using a personal calendar until she was a freshman in college. She still graduated from college with good grades and is a successful young adult who now uses her planner for everything. In short, you may remind your five-year-old every day that he is going to Daddy's on Friday, and he will still be genuinely shocked when Daddy shows up at the door.

Plans for sharing equal time work better when children are older and somewhat more independent. If you and your coparent are intent on sharing equal time with the children, you can make it work, but both parents must be willing to make sacrifices, be flexible, and cooperate. Parents who are overly concerned with whether each parent has exactly equal time should not attempt it. If you decide a 50-50 parenting time split is best for your children, consider a one week on, one week off schedule with the exchange on Sunday evening. Do not be tempted to swap the children every other day or every two days; that sort of schedule not only invites chaos for everyone but also can do lasting harm to your children. If you share the children's time, each parent should have a mid-week dinner visit with the children during the other parent's week. An equal time-sharing schedule requires at least one organized parent and that you have reached the point where you can communicate with the other parent politely. A lot happens in seven days of homework, practices, appointments, clubs, play dates, games, and lessons. It also means being willing to drive the forgotten favorite toy or blanket to the other parent's house and ensuring the homework, science or art project, sports equipment, and musical instruments all make it to the right place at the right time.

There are decisions both parents should be involved with, and child care is one of those critical decisions. It might be tempting to make your own arrangements during your parenting time, but ideally, your child should have only one day care provider. Understandably, it's not always possible to have a single provider, particularly if you and your spouse work odd shifts or have rotating days off. Still, just as your kids need consistent parenting time, they need a consistent caregiver when you are working.

There are lots of questions to ask when deciding about child care. Should your child care provider be someone in an in-home situation, or should the children be cared for in a commercial day care facility? Cost is always a factor; private day cares may be less expensive and homier, and facilities may cost more. Home day cares aren't always licensed, while the state licenses facilities and ensures their employees are qualified and have passed background checks and drug tests. No parent wants to get a call to pick up their child because the babysitter has just been arrested for locking her charges in closets while she dashed out to hit the tanning salon and get her nails done. And no, I didn't make that up, so do your homework and trust your gut.

When you and your spouse negotiate a parenting plan, remember that families are dynamic beasts, and they change and evolve rapidly. Humans tend to assume things will always be what they are now when nothing could be further from the truth. People change jobs, remarry, have other children, divorce, move away, move back, get sick, become disabled, and start businesses. Ask parents who have been coparenting for a few years, and they will tell you they tossed out their original plan a long time ago. One size does not fit all, and the schedule will change as your children grow. The parenting time arrangement that worked when your children were in elementary school won't still work when they're teenagers who drive themselves to and from school and part-time jobs.

HOLIDAY PARENTING-TIME CONSIDERATIONS

Holiday parenting time is filled with emotion and expectation; there are your family traditions, your spouse's family traditions, and the traditions you were hoping to make together with your children. Every year, phone calls began pouring into my office just before a major holiday (invariably at 4:30 p.m. on a Friday) with concerns about upcoming holiday parenting time. My best advice is this: if you are mid-divorce during a holiday, be prepared to be flexible. And yes, I do know that you are likely thinking, "If this book tells me to be flexible one more time, I'm going to see if I can score it in the trash can from the three-point-line." Noted, but unless you have a court order or are willing to head for the courthouse (and had the foresight to file your motion and get a court date three months ago), you need to be realistic.

You have an ex who is angry and bitter this year and might screw with your holiday time. When you negotiate the terms of your final divorce, you will outline the holiday plan for all future years. If your family celebrates Christmas Eve and your former spouse's family always has Christmas breakfast, you might easily write that into your plan.

If you always join your family in Los Angeles or Cape Cod for New Year's, ask for that. If you always attend a family reunion at Grandpa's lake house over the Fourth of July, write that into your plan, but be willing to give the other parent the same consideration in return. If you and your spouse are of different faiths, respect one another's beliefs and do not put your child in the position of having to choose. Don't try to use the holiday schedule to limit your child's participation in the other parent's faith, even if you don't like it. Many people approach the plan by agreeing to alternate the holidays in odd and even years. Table 9.1 details a holiday parenting-time plan.

Table 9.1. Holiday Parenting-Time Plan

Holiday	Parent A	Parent B
Winter Vacation	Even Years	Odd Years
Thanksgiving	Odd Years	Even Years
Easter	Even Years	Odd Years
Memorial Day	Odd Years	Even Years
Fourth of July	Even Years	Odd Years
Labor Day	Odd Years	Even Years
Halloween	Even Years	Odd Years
Spring Break	Odd Years	Even Years
Children's Birthday	Even Years	Odd Years

Parents treat the winter break differently, depending on traditions and plans, and much depends upon the holiday schedule in your children's school district. Courts often order that holiday parenting time follows the local school calendar, even if your child is not attending because they are too young or homeschooled. Some families split the break, exchanging the children on the day after Christmas. Depending on the school schedule, this can result in one parent having more time than the other. If you decide to split the break, the odd/even pattern will apply to which parent gets the first half of the holiday, including Christmas Eve and Christmas Day, and which parent receives the potentially longer second portion. Some parents prefer to alternate the entire break because the longer span makes travel over the holidays easier. The Thanksgiving holiday should include Thanksgiving Thursday and the Friday, Saturday, and Sunday of Thanksgiving week. Fourth of July is a bit of an outlier since the day of the week it falls on changes every year. Often parents agree to alternate the holiday on the odd and even schedule so that no matter what day the holiday falls on, the parent has the child from noon until after the fireworks.

Parents can share the summer break from school in many ways. Much also depends on the school calendar. In districts where they observe a year-round school schedule, your school breaks will differ from the traditional schedule. Some parents choose to keep the same every-other-weekend schedule through the summer. Each parent also gets two weeks of uninterrupted vacation time—the parents alternate who picks their two weeks first each year on the same odd and even schedule. Most plans call for the parent choosing first to identify their dates by May 1 of the year so that the other parent can make their summer plans. Other parents opt to change parenting time during the summer to a one-week-on and one-week-off schedule. Your own choices will depend on work schedules, vacation plans, and the children's summer activities.

If you have an every-other-weekend schedule during the non-holiday time, you should also decide when the regular every-other-weekend schedule resumes and if the pattern restarts after a holiday or continues on the same alternating way. It makes a difference for a parent trying to synchronize their parenting schedule with work or other children's parenting schedule. I've included a sample parenting plan with this chapter. I recommend you download some blank calendar pages and sketch out the schedule so you can visualize it. Go out at least three years and make each parent's time a different color to identify patterns and find gaps. In most cases, you will find any differences in how much time either parent gets averages out over two or three years.

HELP WITH COPARENTING

You and your spouse know your children and your family situation best. That makes you the most qualified to make decisions for your family. Still, sometimes it just isn't possible because there's too much baggage or too much damage for you to approach such an emotional subject as time with your children rationally. Sometimes you need help. Help can come in many forms; you might employ a mediator, a parenting-time coordinator, or in extreme cases, a custody evaluator.

If you choose to use a mediator, educate yourself about the mediation process. We'll examine mediation in depth in chapter 18. There are many types of mediators, and often, individual states don't mandate qualifications for divorce mediators. Lawyers, therapists, and other mental health professionals may all offer mediation. If you mediate child custody and parenting time, a therapist or mental health professional could be the best choice. But mediation can be tricky, and you want an experienced mediator who knows the law and has a calm but firm demeanor. A good mediator's first job is to manage the power in the room during a session because no relationship is ever an exact balance of power. The mediator will walk you through each part of the parenting plan and help you compromise on areas in dispute.

Parents also sometimes employ a parenting coordinator. Unlike a mediator, whose work is finished when you reach an agreement, parenting coordinators help you implement your parenting plan and have an ongoing relationship with you, your former spouse, and your children. A parenting coordinator is especially helpful in high-conflict divorces. The parenting coordinator acts as the central hub for communication and coordination, limiting the necessity for you to communicate directly with your former spouse. Again, qualifications and credentials can vary, so shop around and interview potential candidates. At a minimum, your parenting coordinator will help iron out scheduling problems, help you establish the annual schedule of vacations and holidays, work out transportation arrangements, and help with planning appointments and extracurricular activities. Some parenting coordinators are comfortable supervising the physical exchange from one parent to the other. The coordinator can also help arrange when and how each parent will attend an appointment or activity.

I once had a client with a disabled child. The parents could not agree on their son's medical care, diet, physical therapy, or education. We found a retired nurse to act as their parenting coordinator. She helped the parents manage the scheduling and supervised exchanges. She also helped the parents cooperate on the child's care details, including his dietary needs and medical appointments.

Parenting coordinators charge by the hour, like lawyers. If the parents agree to split the coordinator's fee equally, there is a danger that one parent may run up the bill by contacting the coordinator too much. To avoid this, parents should agree that each parent will pay for their use of the coordinator's time so that they each pay only for the services they use. The cost of conferences with the parenting coordinator when both parents are present should be split equally.

Your coordinator must keep detailed records so that each parent knows what they are paying for. As an added benefit, if litigation becomes necessary, each parent has a history of how and when they communicated with the coordinator.

You may think hiring a parenting coordinator is overkill (and it may be for your specific situation), but let me illustrate with a story: A husband and wife were divorced. They haggled for years over their son's custody and found fault with the other parent at every turn. They spent tens of thousands of dollars on attorneys and evaluations and court hearings. Nothing either parent could do would satisfy the other. The parents were still haggling and appealing when their son, then a young teenager, was killed in a tragic accident. The parents then spent the next fifteen years fighting over possession of his cremated remains. I like to think a parenting coordinator might have helped defuse some of their hostility.

Parents often try to use their children to control their ex-spouses, even when they don't realize they're doing it. You hurt your child more than you hurt the other parent when you do that, so here are a few dos and don'ts.

DO communicate with the other parent in a neutral and business-like way and only about things relevant to the children.

DON'T use the children as go-betweens to communicate with the other parent.

DO encourage your child's contact with the other parent.

DO give the other parent information about where you will be and what you will be doing if you plan to take the child out of town.

DO answer your phone when the other parent calls.

DO return calls and answer texts and e-mails promptly.

DON'T demand that the other parent use you as the babysitter for the child during their time. Parents are responsible for caring for their children during their time, including making babysitting arrangements. Requiring the other parent to use you as a babysitter is just a roundabout way of insisting that they tell you any time they have social plans.

DO be flexible whenever possible and trade weekends willingly.

DON'T plan fun and exciting things with the children on the other parent's weekend and then tell the children it's the other parent's fault when they can't go.

Having a special needs child can be its own built-in circle of guilt-hell. Add the feelings of shame and failure that follow any divorce, and you have a perfect recipe for anxiety and depression. If you are in this situation, get to a therapist *immediately* because single parenting able children is challenging; being the lone parent of a special-needs child can be paralyzing. There is so much more to meeting a disabled child's needs and so many more people involved. In one of my cases, we had to reserve extra space to have meetings because the care team couldn't fit at my office. There were school representatives, teachers, bus drivers, a nutritionist, developmental disability services personnel, daily care aides, physical and occupational therapists, and physicians.

In another of my cases, my client and her former husband had two children with a rare genetic disorder. The disorder caused the children to be physically and intellectually handicapped to the extent they required around-the-clock care. Both parents were utterly devoted to caring for these children, who, at ages eleven and thirteen, needed the same care as six-month-old babies. The children exceeded their expected lifespans by years, thanks to their parents' tender attention, but when one of the children died, each of the parents bitterly blamed the other. Their grief found an outlet in an exhausting years-long battle over the surviving child's custody and parenting time.

All children need to see the doctor now and then, and while urgent needs are pretty easy to call, elective medical procedures can raise more questions. Should your toddler have ear tubes surgically implanted to help chronic ear infections? Should your child's ears be pierced? Should your child be medicated for hyperactivity or receive treatment with growth hormones? Should you let your sixteen-year-old get their first tattoo? And how pissed off will you be if your ex-spouse allows your sixteen-year-old to get their first tattoo without consulting you?

It's here that we need to talk about that trust thing again. It's so important I've devoted an entire chapter to the subject, so please review chapter 8. Marriages don't end because people love and trust each other. They end because the trust between partners breaks down. *Webster's* dictionary defines trust as "firm belief in the character, strength, or truth of someone or something." Here you are, expected to entrust the thing you love most in the world, your child, to a person you wouldn't trust any farther than you can throw them. Rebuilding trust with that person is the single most important and most challenging thing you must do. You must earn your ex-spouse's trust and allow your ex to earn yours.

Complications can arise about custody and parenting time when one parent is not a U.S. citizen. In some situations, the children are even granted dual citizenship. The United States does not recognize dual citizenship, but many other countries do. For example, the mother is a U.S. citizen; the father is a French citizen in the United States on a marriage visa. The children are born in the United States and are considered U.S. citizens. However, if the father registers the children with the French government, France also considers them French citizens. This situation can be problematic if the other country where the children have citizenship is one with different or stricter laws on custody. For example, in many Middle Eastern countries, mothers have no custodial rights to their children if they divorce. That means during an acrimonious divorce, a father could travel to his native country with his children, then claim sole custody and withhold the children from their mother under his country's laws.

In 1980, a treaty called the Hague Convention on the Civil Aspects of International Child Abduction was created. Signatory countries have enacted legal processes for parents to recover children who have been taken by a parent. But while more than one hundred countries have signed the treaty, the Hague Conference has no mandate and no power to assist in individual abduction cases. And even more unfortunate, many of the worst offenders are not signatories to the Convention. If you are divorcing a spouse who is not a citizen or maintains dual citizenship with a country that gives custody preference to their citizens, you must take special precautions. The most important thing you can do is get and keep possession of the children's passports and birth certificates. You should also insist on a provision in your divorce judgment that orders the children to remain in the United States, even though such an order may limit your ability to vacation with the children internationally. A provision in your decree can help prove your intentions, but it only binds you and your former spouse. It does not bind government officials in any country, including the United States.

FINDING COMMON GROUND

It's inevitable that you and your former spouse will disagree about your children. Still, picking your battles is critical. For example, if you are of a religious faith that does not believe in blood transfusions, that may be the most crucial issue for you. If, on the other hand, your child's participation in a sport or activity is paramount to you, you may prioritize that. Let's discuss some considerations surrounding each of the more important parental decisions.

Education

Parents often differ on education, and their own educational experiences usually inform their opinions. Will your child attend public or private school? What goes into that decision may be much more than just privilege and the ability to pay. Many parents see a private religious education as a balance to the secular, sexualized, and worldly environment of popular culture. Others feel they do their children a disservice by insulating them from the real world. Some parents think a private school with an alternative learning style might better meet their child's individual needs, while some want their children to learn to live in the larger, diverse world. Then there are the parents who just want to be in charge. When deciding about education, it's essential to examine your motives. I have had clients insist that their children attend private school merely to increase the financial burden on the other parent. Educational decisions should always be motivated by your children's needs and their best interests. Let's review **Rule 1**: *Whatever this shit is, it belongs to you. Don't make your shit your children's shit. Ever.*

Following the education upheavals surrounding COVID-19, some parents continue to work from home and have opted to continue their children's distance learning, turning working parents into teachers. Just when you thought it couldn't get any shittier, you may find yourself a single parent in the middle of a divorce, working from home while also overseeing your children's daily school participation. You might be right; it can't get shittier. I'm sure you don't want to hear me suggest that you need to enlist the help of your coparent, but maybe you do. Let me put it this way: whatever you do, you need a plan. If your children's other parent is also working from home, perhaps you can establish a schedule that allows each of you to balance work and the children's schooling. Most parents are not trained teachers; if you aren't, then every time you teach your child something, you'll have to learn first. It also takes time to learn the technology and each teacher's expectations and routine. It may be easier if two people tackle it, even if the two people don't like each other much at the moment.

Religion

I've had many cases where faith was a point of contention. I've had cases where one spouse left or was excluded from the family's faith, and I've had cases where one person's newfound faith caused irreparable harm to a marriage. It's true that, sometimes, a thing that is supposed to make people better becomes the hill they want to die on. Remember, it's your divorce, not the Crusades. Don't make your children feel they have to choose or that they're going to hell if they do. Your faith can be a haven for you and your children during your divorce. It comes down to that trust thing again. Trust that your higher power knows what everyone needs.

Medical Treatment

Parents sometimes have sharp disagreements about medical decisions for their children. As a rule, the custodial parent makes the medical decisions. If the parents have joint custody, they consult one another on the treatment choices. Most parents have healthy children and can make decisions rationally, but what happens if the child is medically fragile, or there are other factors at play?

I once represented a father whose ex-wife had custody of their two daughters. One of the reasons my client and his wife divorced was because she had become involved with a pseudo-religious group that refused all medical intervention, treating even serious illnesses only with prayer. She refused to permit the children, who both had a chronic genetic illness, to be treated with antibiotics. The situation is different when both parents choose to raise their children in a faith that may not believe in medical treatment. In general, the court will not interfere in a couple's decisions about medical treatment for their children if the parents agree. Still, the parents' agreement doesn't guarantee that medical providers won't involve the local child protective service if they believe there is a risk of harm to the child.

Relationships with Other Family Members

Divorce doesn't just end a marriage, it fractures family relationships, and your families are also figuring out how to navigate this new terrain. New stepparents and grandparents can be your rocks during divorce, and like rocks, they can either provide stability or contribute to a landslide.

The U.S. Supreme Court decided a case called *Troxel v. Granville*;[1] the case placed limitations on third parties' rights, including grandparents and stepparents. In decisions about custody and parenting time, biological parents take precedence over third parties unless the third party can prove that the birth parents are unwilling or unable to parent the children. It's not enough that the grandparents have a nicer home or better jobs. To be awarded custody of a grandchild over a biological parent's objection, the grandparents must prove the birth parents are unwilling or unfit to care for the children. That's a high bar. To make it higher, the court also set the standard of proof at clear and convincing.

A note about the legal standard of proof: the court must apply a standard of proof in every decision. In most civil cases, the standard of proof is by a *preponderance of the evidence* (think of it as 51 percent of the evidence supports your case). Some civil matters require the higher standard of proof of by *clear and convincing evidence* (more like 75 percent).

The highest standard, *beyond a reasonable doubt* (99 percent), is reserved for criminal cases. In a custody case between the children's legal parents, one parent must prove by a preponderance of the evidence (51 percent or more likely than not) that it's in the children's best interest that custody is awarded to them. In a third-party custody case, the person seeking custody must prove by clear and convincing evidence (75 percent) that the biological parents are unwilling or unfit and then prove that it's in the child's best interest the third party is awarded custody of the children.

The standard is somewhat lower when it comes to awarding a third party visitation with children. However, a third party must still show by a preponderance of the evidence (51 percent) that they have a close ongoing relationship with the child. While the *Troxel* case was influential in establishing that biological parents' rights are superior to anyone else under the Constitution, before the legalization of gay marriage, *Troxel* caused some questionable outcomes for same-sex couples with children. Chapter 12 discusses some of the legal complications surrounding gay parents and the use of assisted reproduction.

Ultimately, when it comes to custody and parenting time, it doesn't matter so much what you call it as how you do it. If you're ever tempted to withhold time with the children from your former spouse or threaten to challenge custody to gain the upper hand or punish your ex, I hope this chapter has dissuaded you. If not, let me state clearly: your children are not possessions or pawns; they are human beings who are doing the hard work of growing and learning. Their capacity to understand complex adult emotions is limited, so it's your job to create the best environment for them. If that doesn't convince you, consider this: your child may blame you later in life for the conflict you create during their childhood. Remember that thing we said as kids? "I'm rubber, and you're glue. Whatever you say and do bounces off me and sticks to you."

10

PARENTING ON
THE NEW FRONTIER

THE FATHER'S CHANGING ROLE

If your parents were divorced, you might remember how your mom called all the shots, and your dad just showed up Sunday, took you bowling, got you jazzed on Red Vines and root beer, and then dropped you home so your mom could make you do your homework. Not today.

Fathers expect and are expected to coparent. In case you've missed it, there are baby changing tables in the men's restrooms and dads are arranging play dates. When our daughter was born, my husband and I decided he would be the parent to stay home with her. Our daughter's life was deeply enriched by having a father who played that role in her life, and neither of us liked it when people called him "Mr. Mom" or asked if he was "babysitting" his child. Fathers are integral parts of their children's emotional growth. Experts tell us that having two loving, functional parents is much more important than whether those parents live in the same home. Many long-term longitudinal studies of children from divorced families report that children of divorce suffer from increased anxiety and depression, fare worse in the workplace, and are less likely to finish high school or pursue college. But it's important to point out that these studies historically captured children whose fathers took the more traditional bowling-alley-dad role. Studies that measure the level of parental engagement after divorce indicate that children whose parents are both able to stay meaningfully involved with them fare far better. Parents who can set aside hostility and encourage healthy relationships between their children and the other parent raise emotionally healthy kids.

Children do best when they have a home base. They need consistency and stability. They learn that the world is a place they can trust because they learn to trust both of you. They trust that you will always put their needs first, be there when you say you will, keep your word, and come when called, and that trust gives them security and confidence. Allowing them to love each of you tells them that you also trust them. When I began practicing in the early 1990s, we lawyers focused on making parenting time equal. We reasoned that equality would force fathers to be more engaged and require them to ensure their children did their homework and brushed their teeth. Lawyers aren't psychologists, and before long, experts began telling us how wrong we were. Like most of life, our approach emphasized quality over quantity and substance over style.

States began recognizing that fathers were spending more time with children and decided that child support should reflect that. Many states started factoring the time each parent spends with the child into support calculations. Indeed, a parent should pay less support if they spend more time with the children. However, the flip side is, some parents push for more parenting time just to pay less support and don't take into consideration what is best for their child. Here is the perfect place to introduce **Rule 5**: *Kids before cash.* Do what's best for your children before you consider the monetary cost or benefit to you. Sure, you may be able to lower your child support if your child is with you every other week rather than two weekends per month, but if that means parking the child with your boyfriend's teenaged daughter every day while you go to work, how does that benefit your child?

Not all parents fight to see their children. One of the most challenging questions any lawyer gets is this: "How do I *make* my ex see the children?" If you're in that position, try your best to communicate with your former spouse. If the children frequently ask when they will see your ex, tell your ex that they are asking. You may also want to think about whether you are part of the problem. Noncustodial parents sometimes give up when they view the fight to see their children as unwinnable. Parenting time is for the benefit of your children, so make it as easy as possible for your former spouse to see your children. I know it's hard. Do it anyway. You will feel like it's not fair or like the other parent is taking advantage of you. Do it anyway. Never use parenting time to control or punish the other parent. Don't forget **Rule 1**: *Whatever this shit is, it belongs to you. Don't make your shit your children's shit. Ever.* If you're making it uncomfortable and challenging for your child to see the other parent, it may rebound on you. Your child may blame you for their lack of relationship with the other parent. Likewise, if you decide not to see your children because it's too difficult to deal with your ex, your children won't love you less; they will blame themselves and love themselves less. Later, when you come to your senses and want a relationship with them, they may also decide that they don't need you in their lives.

PARENTING GUIDES

There are many excellent parenting guides and philosophies out there. The shelf at the bookstore stretches for miles. One I recommend is *Parenting with Love and Logic*, written by Foster W. Cline, MD, and Jim Fay. These are tried and proven ideas that have stood the test of time. Their program focuses on building trust and confidence by allowing the natural consequences of a person's choices to teach life lessons.

I describe the idea this way: your six-year-old gets up in the morning for school. It's winter, and there's snow on the ground. As he is getting ready, you suggest your child wear their warm coat. They insist on the lighter—but infinitely cooler—Spider-Man coat. You have a choice: fight this battle, or let life teach the lesson about choices and consequences. You mentally run through the possible consequences. What's the worst thing that might happen? Your child might get cold at recess and have to go inside early. Hmm. You can live with that. So, you let them trot off to school in the Spider-Man jacket. When your child gets home, you ask, "How was school?" You ask open-ended questions, like, "How was recess? Who did you play with?" The child volunteers that recess was fun, but they got cold and had to go in early. You might be tempted here to reinforce that you were right all along, with an "I told you so." Don't.

Instead, you do what the authors of the book call "locking in empathy." That means you say something like, "I'm sorry, that must have been hard," and leave the conversation right there. Now, when the following morning arrives, you'll find no fight over which jacket your child will wear. Instead, they'll ask if they can have mittens, too. Cline and Fay's book is humorous and easy to read, and it gives lots of concrete examples of how to use their techniques. There are many YouTube videos of seminars on the subject and a podcast called *The Love and Logic Podcast*. There are hundreds—maybe even thousands—of books about parenting. *Love and Logic* is only one scheme for parenting, and it may not work for everyone. The reason I bring *Love and Logic* up here is twofold. First, the ideas have worked for millions of parents. Second, the techniques work just as well on ex-spouses as on children. Allowing your ex to make their own choices and learn from the consequences while you lock in the empathy may be some of the most satisfying communications you will have with them.

PARENTING YOUR CHILD THROUGH TRANSITIONS

Your children will still struggle with the transition between households even if you and your ex have an excellent relationship because children don't like change; kids are busy learning to trust, and rapid-fire change doesn't create trust. Parents can do some things to ease the stress of the transitions. First, choose a parenting plan that minimizes switching between households, particularly with children younger than middle school. Then, develop a transition routine, like a bedtime routine, to help your child move from one phase of their day to another. When your child has an established bedtime routine, it helps them slow from the day's busy pace and prepare for sleep. Transition routines serve that exact purpose. They help your child shift gears from one home to the other. Routine and consistency lessen your child's fear and anxiety about change. Begin by reminding the child they are going to the other parent and enlisting their help in getting ready. Be consistent about how you and your child prepare. Do you always make sure your child has dinner before the exchange? You might choose to serve the same food before each exchange or take time for a cuddle and read a transition book.

There is a charming children's book I've been recommending for years. It's called *The Kissing Hand*, written by Audrey Penn. The story features a raccoon parent and child. The child is apprehensive about going to school for the first time. To reassure the child they will always be there, the parent takes the child's hand and plants a kiss on its palm. The parent tells the child that their hand will keep the kiss until it is needed. Then, the child only needs to hold the kiss to its face to feel the parent's love. I recommend that clients read the book with their child just before it's time for the other parent to pick the child up. I also recommend that you buy two copies and encourage the other parent to do the same. Kisses can be "sent" through the phone when the child is away from the parent.

Children also benefit from a transition buddy. It can be a toy, a blanket, or a stuffed animal that is always with them, no matter which house they're at. The buddy becomes a touchstone, an outward and comforting manifestation of their ability to handle the transition. When my daughter was young, I traveled for work more than she liked. We hit upon a strategy that worked for us. Before I left, she would help me pack a little black-and-white stuffed skunk we named "Stinky" in my bag. Stinky went with me to keep me company when I had to go on a trip. Upon arrival, the first thing I did was snap a photo of Stinky on my hotel bed and send it to her. Likewise, if she went somewhere overnight, Stinky went with her, and she sent me a picture. Years later, when I woke after some minor surgery, I found Stinky tucked in with me.

These transition strategies are especially beneficial if parents have different parenting styles. While you were married, you probably could mesh your styles; now that you are divorced, the differences may have become glaringly apparent. When your former spouse tells you how to do things, it may feel like they are trying to control the way you parent. Step back a moment and remember that you're trying to both build a trusting relationship around parenting with your former spouse and encourage confidence in your child around the transitions. While you might not trust your former spouse with your heart, you still need to be able to trust that the other parent will act in your children's best interest. Here are some suggestions that can help build that trust:

Return the clothes and toys. Nothing is more frustrating for a parent than to buy their child a new pair of shoes or a new toy and never see it again. Unless you and your coparent agree otherwise, the child's clothes and toys belong to them and should go with them when they move between houses. When possible, do the laundry and return the clothing clean.

Return all medicine and sports equipment. If your child is taking medication, be sure you keep a log of how much you give and when. If your child plays a sport, make sure their gear goes with them. If you really want to score points, make sure the sweaty uniforms go home clean. And by the way, don't let anyone tell you girls who play sports don't smell just as bad as the boys. I speak from experience when I tell you they do.

Return your child prepared. Most parenting-time transitions occur in the early evening, often on Sunday. If you are the returning parent, make sure you return the children ready for the following day. That means feed them dinner, make sure they finish their homework, and bathe them if possible. What parent wouldn't appreciate their child coming home fed, bathed, and already in their pajamas?

Share transportation. Take turns with pickups and deliveries or agree that the parent receiving the child will pick up. If you visit your child from a distance, share transportation costs when you can, and if the exchange requires driving, agree to meet halfway.

Make transitions easy. I know I've said this before, but it bears repeating. If you have a schedule where a parent picks the child up at school, respect that your child may not want to telegraph it to their schoolmates. Find a way to exchange the children's belongings privately. I once shared office space with a divorced dad. Every other weekend I would come back from lunch on Friday to find his child's suitcase and ski gear stacked in the hall where her mother had delivered it.

Share household routines. Keep the routine similar in both households. It will take some coordination with the other parent, and it might be uncomfortable. Do it anyway. Keep homework routines, bedtimes, and rules about screen time as consistent as possible. Observe rules about what media the child is allowed in both homes. If one parent says PG movies only, don't let the child watch PG-13 movies at your house. If your child really wants to see a film that's outside the agreed-to rating, talk it over with the other parent. Perhaps agree that one or both of you will screen the movie in advance. It's about more than just keeping the peace. Maintaining consistent rules in both households reinforces your child's trust in both of you and teaches them the world is a reliable place. That, in turn, builds your child's confidence. **Establish rules regarding social media and the internet**. Yep, it's scary out there, and if you're like most parents, you only see the top one-third of the iceberg. The internet is an area where you and your former spouse must be on the same page, even if it means you have to compromise on other things. Give in on PG-13 movies if it means your former spouse agrees to monitor your children's social media activity. It's also critical that you have frank conversations with your children about the dangers that lurk on the internet and how to use social media responsibly and safely.

First, there was Myspace and Facebook, then Instagram, and suddenly there's Snapchat, WhatsApp, TikTok, and dozens more that appear every month. Your kid may say you're intruding on their privacy, but it's reasonable to look at your child's phone, know which applications are on it, and require some kind of access. As your children get older, keeping track of what's on their phone may be less necessary and may seem more intrusive for both you and your child. Parents I've known have had success balancing their child's privacy with their need to assure their child is safe by asking the child to write down the username and password for every social media platform account and the password for their phone and seal it in an envelope. The parent keeps the envelope with the understanding that if the child abuses their social media or posts offensive or bullying content, the parent will open the envelope and use the contents to delete every account. Changing passwords also will have consequences that may include losing the use of their phone. Many parents also require that their child add them as a friend on any social media platform they use.

Be flexible. There will be times when you will have to go out of your way to make your parenting plan work. There will be a forgotten homework project, medicine, or the all-important blankie that must be delivered to the other parent. There will be family and work emergencies that will require the other parent's patience and cooperation.

Never schedule vacations or activities on the other parent's time without permission. If you think your child absolutely must play baseball, learn ballet, or act in a play, and some or all of those activities occur on the other parent's time, make sure that the other parent is on board. Be specific. Who is taking the child to practice, and who will attend the games? If the child has a game on the other parent's time, may you still attend? Can you bring your new partner? Will either parent act as a coach? If your child gets invited to a birthday party on the other parent's time, only RSVP if the other parent agrees, and coordinate who will be responsible for buying the birthday present. Your child does not have to attend every event they get invited to. And *never* make the other parent the bad guy if they say no. I don't know how many times I've heard about a parent saying to a child, "I was going to take you on a fun trip next weekend, but it's your mom's weekend, and she won't let you go." Most parenting plans spell out a vacation schedule that parallels the school holidays. Plan vacations according to the written schedule and discuss scheduling with the other parent first. If there is an event that you would like to attend with your child, discuss it with the other parent first, and coordinate a plan, exchange time if needed, and don't tell your child, "You're going to be a flower girl in Auntie Sylvia's wedding if your daddy will let you." Don't take children out of school for vacation unless the other parent agrees.

Use helmets and child safety seats and boosters. Your children have a right to be safe. They must be in a safety seat or booster when driving in a car, and that car must be driven by a sober, licensed, and insured driver. Each parent should designate others that might transport the child, as long as that driver is safe. You don't have the right to forbid your ex's parents or relatives from picking the child up just because you don't like them. Likewise, if your former spouse has a new partner who is also a part of your child's life, trying to limit their ability to transport your child is just petty. If your child is horseback riding, skiing, or riding a bicycle, an all-terrain vehicle, a snowmobile, a skateboard, or a scooter, they should be wearing a helmet and, if appropriate, elbow and knee pads. If you are riding a bike or skiing with your child, set a good example and wear a helmet yourself. If your child is on a jet ski, in a boat, or water skiing or wakeboarding, they must wear a lifejacket.

Deal with risky business. Just as you and your former spouse have different parenting styles, you probably have different tolerances for risk. As a rule, mothers are more risk averse. The decision of whether your child will play contact sports like football or ride motorcycles, all-terrain vehicles, or horses must be a mutual one. It's not fair to force one parent to accept a risk they are not comfortable with; be sure you are on the same page before you let your child engage in risky behavior. I've seen more than one parenting relationship damaged beyond repair when their child was injured because one parent allowed a child to do something dangerous.

COPARENTING AND ADDICTION AND MENTAL HEALTH ISSUES

Coparenting with someone who suffers from addiction or mental health issues is one of the most challenging situations. How do you walk the tightrope of encouraging a relationship between your child and their parent while still protecting the child? Millions of parents are struggling alongside you. First, I suggest that you get involved with Al-Anon, and if your children are old enough, they should attend Alateen. These organizations can help you understand your former spouse's addiction and teach you to set proper boundaries; both are skills that codependent spouses and children struggle with. It's vital work. It will help you to help your children and improve your communication with your coparent, and it will help you grow and prepare for a future partner. It can be exceptionally hard to coparent with someone who has a personality disorder and insists on putting your children in the middle or using them to manipulate you. Remember **Rule 3**: *Never confront a person who is irrational, intoxicated, or both*. Remember, the healthier you are, the easier it will be to set boundaries with your ex. Educating yourself on coping strategies by working with your own therapist is imperative if you coparent with a person struggling with mental illness and addiction.

Let me illustrate with a story. I once met with a client who wanted custody of her grandchildren because their mother, her daughter, struggled with addiction. When my client described the situation to me, what emerged was one of the most lopsided, codependent relationships I had ever seen. My client grew up in a severely dysfunctional, alcoholic family. As a response, my client abstained entirely from alcohol and expected her children to do the same. Her daughter rebelled and began using drugs and alcohol as a teenager. The daughter had two children with two different men, neither of which had remained in her children's lives. My client's response was the one she'd learned in her family of origin, where she had been a parentified and codependent caregiver. She stepped in to care for her grandchildren while accommodating the daughter's every demand because she believed she was helping. Remember our Rube Goldberg machine? Hers was huge, complex, and exhausting. The tipping point came when my client paid for the daughter to marry her drug dealer in an expensive destination wedding. The wedding weekend devolved into a drama-filled nightmare that ended with the daughter blaming my client for everything terrible that had ever happened to her and forbidding her ever to see her grandchildren again.

Understanding, as I do, the limitations of grandparent rights, I helped her brainstorm a different approach and sent her to Al-Anon. There she learned a new and healthier way to relate to her daughter. Three months later, when we met again, she had gained new confidence in herself, and she and her daughter had begun talking. She had just had her first weekend visit with her grandchildren, and her daughter had agreed to try counseling with her. She not only was learning new ways to communicate but also learning how to draw boundaries. She was learning when to stand back and let life teach the lesson. It was hard, but my client discovered how much happier she was when she did. Her daughter had not yet admitted and confronted her addiction, but my client now understood it was her daughter's responsibility and not hers.

A couple of years later, I ran into my former client in a store. She was with her daughter and grandchildren. My former client proudly told me her daughter had voluntarily gone into a residential treatment program the year before and was now doing well. The daughter had rid herself of the drug dealer husband and was staying sober and attending college, and she and the children were living with my client. Not every story has this kind of happy ending, but the odds substantially increase when you do your part.

There are times when keeping your children safe, even from their other parent, must be your top priority. There are instances when you can and should demand that your former spouse not use drugs or alcohol while the children are in their care and when you should ensure they don't through drug or alcohol testing. These solutions aren't the appropriate response when your ex parties too much on the weekends.

It is a solution you must demand for the "my ex drinks all the time and drives with my children in the car" or the "my ex blacks out and wakes up later in another county" scenarios. The testing can be expensive, and you will probably need a court order to force your ex-spouse to comply. Let's talk a bit about how testing works. Drug and alcohol testing is not the end-all, but you can use it as an effective tool. The tests detect the substance or the byproducts of metabolizing the substance in a person's urine. Alcohol and most street drugs are water soluble. That means they require water to be metabolized, and the body excretes them fairly quickly, generally in one to three days.

On the other hand, THC, the psychoactive ingredient in marijuana, is fat soluble. It is stored in the fat cells of the body and excreted over time. While water-soluble substances may be out of the body in one to three days, THC can remain in the body for as many as forty-five days as it releases slowly from the person's fat cells. This slow dissipation is what makes the legalization of recreational marijuana so problematic. While there is a direct correlation between the level of alcohol in your bloodstream and your level of intoxication, the same can't be said for marijuana. The recreational use of marijuana may be legal in your jurisdiction, but driving under its influence is not. The dilemma comes because science hasn't yet developed a reliable test to measure when a person is intoxicated by marijuana.

If your former spouse is suffering from addiction, requiring that they take drug tests can be an effective way to ensure they are not using while parenting the children. As I've explained, it's not foolproof. Having your former spouse test before parenting time begins can discourage their use; requiring them to test after the children's parenting time can prove whether they stuck to the court's order while the children were in their care. Over the years, I have found testing after parenting time the most helpful, especially if the judge has also ordered that parenting time may be suspended if the addicted parent tests positive following their time with the children. In those situations, if parenting time is suspended because of drug use, I insist that, before parenting time resumes, the addicted parent provides proof they are actively participating in substance abuse treatment and provides at least three consecutive clean drug tests.

To be clear: suspending parenting time is hard on your children, so it should be a last resort. Stopping parenting time is not your chance to punish what you perceive to be your spouse's lack of character or willpower. Addiction is a disease. We don't punish people for being diabetic. Still, we expect them to take responsibility for managing their condition, and we do expect them to accept the consequences when they don't.

Another option for protecting children is to ask the judge to order that an adult supervise the other parent's parenting time. Supervised time isn't ideal, but it's better than nothing. A therapist or other provider can do supervision. Some communities offer supervision through an agency. Supervision is appropriate when the supervised parent cannot safely and responsibly parent. Supervision is necessary if a parent is violent, has sexually abused their own or other children, or can't refrain from drugs or alcohol during parenting time.

In some instances, the child may be safe with the parent, but the exchange requires supervision because there has been domestic violence between the partners, and they need a neutral, no-contact exchange. Those same agencies often offer that service. There is sometimes a small fee for supervising parenting time or exchanges. Couples who employ a parenting coordinator can also choose one who will supervise exchanges.

SUSPECTED OR CONFIRMED SEXUAL ABUSE

There may be other reasons to limit your former spouse's parenting time. One such situation is when the former spouse or someone in his household has been accused or convicted of sexual misconduct. It's a touchy topic, but to quote author Glennon Doyle in her book *Untamed*, "we can do hard things."[1]

In one case, my client's divorce had been final for about six months when I received a frantic telephone call. Her former spouse was arrested for sexually abusing a neighbor child. The former spouse had remained in the family home, and the victim was good friends with their child. Before the divorce, my client's family and the neighbors had been close. The neighbor child had been to sleepovers with my client's children, both before and after the divorce. She asked me what to do; she couldn't send her child back to that home to visit until we knew the truth.

Judges expect people to follow court orders. In this case, there was a court-ordered parenting plan that allowed the father parenting time every other weekend. My client could not unilaterally suspend the parenting time without a court order. However, because there had been an arrest, a criminal court judge had already forbidden the father from contact with minor children while he was out on bail, including his children. That gave us a window to ask the family court to suspend the father's parenting time. We filed an emergency motion to temporarily suspend his parenting time, pending the criminal charges' resolution. You might be wondering why we only asked for a temporary suspension. It's because although the father was accused of the crime, he was innocent until proven guilty. Filing for a temporary suspension was the right thing, and the judge granted the motion.

My client promptly put her child into therapy, and we waited for the criminal cases to wind through the system. At first, the husband vehemently denied the allegations, but my client was suspicious that he had abused their daughter, too. When a trained investigator gently questioned, the daughter did not disclose anything about her father abusing her. Still, as the investigation moved forward, at least one other child from the neighborhood made disclosures about my client's former spouse. After those revelations, the husband agreed to plead guilty. His guilty plea meant that none of the children had to testify against their abuser.

The former husband served about a year in prison and was released on lengthy parole and a lifetime requirement to register as a sex offender. Shortly after his release, he began demanding parenting time with his children. My client resisted because she was still unsure if her child had been victimized. Fortunately, sex offender parole requires that offenders participate in sex offender treatment and submit to verification polygraph tests. Treatment providers use polygraphs to verify offenders are honest during their years of treatment. Before his first polygraph test, his treatment provider urged him to disclose all of his victims. It was then that he finally admitted he had abused his own daughter while she was likely too young to remember. Following that revelation, the family court judge ordered that the father's parenting time with his child be supervised by professionals indefinitely.

Experts have conflicting opinions about the effectiveness of sex offender treatment. We know that treatment is most effective with juveniles and becomes less effective as the offender ages. Most experts will tell you that the effectiveness of treatment and the recidivism rates vary greatly depending on the offender's age, mental capacity, whether there are co-occurring mental health conditions, and which treatment modality is used. Reestablishing contact between a parent and their child victim should be approached very carefully and thoughtfully.

Sexually abused children are five times more likely to experience depression, suicidal ideation, addiction, poor academic performance, and juvenile delinquency. They are also five times as likely to abuse others sexually.[2] If you believe your former spouse or someone in their household is sexually abusing your children, report your concerns to the police. If your child discloses to you, remain calm and do not question the child in depth. You must leave the questioning up to those who are trained for it because children are suggestible, and improper questioning can destroy crucial evidence. Most jurisdictions have a hybrid medical and law enforcement agency where children receive a physical examination from a doctor. It's important to note that there is rarely physical evidence of the inappropriate sexual contact. A trained investigative specialist will interview the child. Law enforcement personnel sometimes observe the interview with the child through a two-way mirror. Parents are not present during interviews but may be present to comfort an apprehensive child during a medical examination.

Child sexual abuse is a horrendous crime. So is accusing someone of sexually abusing a child when they have not. Those allegations have the power to ruin someone's life. Floating those suspicions as a way to gain the upper hand in a custody fight is despicable, and I've seen it backfire more than once when a judge decided the accusing spouse was lying. The collateral consequences of being labeled as a sex offender are like ripples in water. Identifying your former spouse as a sex offender may interfere with their employment and limit their ability to pay child and spousal support.

It's every parent's responsibility to educate themselves about child abuse. I highly recommend the Darkness to Light program. The organization offers free online training for anyone who has concerns about the abuse of a child. You can find their training materials on their website (d2l.org).

11

THE GRAY MARRIAGE

While much of this book discusses issues that may apply to younger couples and young families, they are not the only ones who divorce. Even long-term marriages sometimes end in divorce, and there are special considerations for divorcing seniors.

People can experience significant and unexpected changes as they age. The changes may be physical, emotional, or psychological. Physical changes can sometimes trigger mental health conditions. A client once came to see me because her husband of many years began behaving erratically. My client discovered that her husband, who had always been shy and financially conservative, started a fictitious life with a woman he'd met online. He convinced his online paramour that he was wealthy and single. After discovering her husband had sent his digital girlfriend an expensive watch for her birthday, my client came to me, asking what measures she could take to protect the life she and her husband had carefully built over the years. She wasn't sure what triggered the change, and my client was hesitant to divorce; she held out some hope that she could convince her husband to get a medical assessment. Unfortunately, the husband was unable to recognize the changes in his behavior, and finally, after several attempts at counseling, my client ended the marriage. With help, she safeguarded her portion of the marital assets from his irresponsible and uncontrolled spending.

In many marriages, one spouse takes charge of the family finances. In long-term marriages, the other spouse may have never managed their own money and may have no idea what they own or how to manage their assets. This situation means that you could find yourself learning budget and finance basics amid the upheaval of your divorce.

Older spouses can become ill or mentally incapacitated. Five million people in the United States have Alzheimer's or dementia, and sixteen million of their family members provide some form of unpaid care for them. This information comes from the Alzheimer's Association, which also estimates the number of people with some form of Alzheimer's dementia will rise to fourteen million by the year 2050.[1] Cases where one spouse develops Alzheimer's disease or other dementia-related conditions are especially challenging. A partner may notice small changes in their spouse but not immediately identify them as a decline in cognitive function. The changes can be subtle shifts in their spouse's personality at first but become the start of a long and sad chapter. It's a time that can be filled with emotional and financial challenges. People with early-onset dementia know something is wrong and, as a result, can become angry, fearful, and suspicious. Under the influence of dementia, even the gentlest of spouses might become physically combative.

If you are living with a spouse who is in cognitive decline, please seek professional help. Begin by having your spouse see a neurologist. Some medications can slow the progression and ease your spouse's anxiety. Next, seek support for yourself. Start individual therapy and join a caregiver support group. It's a critical step. Remember the safety instructions you get on an airplane? "In case of a loss of cabin pressure, oxygen masks will drop from the ceiling. If you are traveling with someone who needs help, secure your mask first." They give that instruction because of our natural inclination to make sure our loved ones are safe first. Realistically, you can't be of any help if you're incapacitated.

As you face what experts have termed "the long goodbye," there are practical decisions to be made. How will you care for your spouse? Is there a point at which you will need outside help with their care? What will that cost, and what financial provisions can you make for both of you? This book is not about financial planning or elder law. If your spouse is diagnosed with the early stages of Alzheimer's or dementia, you must consult with an attorney specializing in elder law as soon as possible. You need someone to help protect your assets and navigate Social Security, Medicare, Medicaid, and the tax consequences of pensions. Many government benefits you may apply for require a "look-back" period to discourage fraud, which means that the sooner you begin planning, the better. The look-back period is intended to prevent people applying for government benefits from giving away or selling assets at less than market value to get their assets below the program's asset limit. It's especially important to consider when one partner needs the support of Medicaid.

Couples who divorce later in life are often on fixed incomes. Your financial outlook is quite different from people who are still active in the workforce. In some instances, older couples may be deciding how to allocate the substantial assets they've accumulated together. In others, they may simply be trying to determine how to support two households on fixed and limited incomes. In either case, you're dealing with a finite pool of assets. We'll talk more about the division of retirement accounts in chapter 17. When you are paying into retirement accounts, they are considered property, but when they reach the point where you are drawing from them, they become income.

There are many possible sources of retirement income. The most common is Social Security. Everyone who pays into Social Security is entitled to draw on it at retirement. The age at which you can draw your Social Security benefit varies depending on the year you were born. As average life expectancies have increased, so has the Social Security retirement age. Typically, Social Security bases the benefit on your past annual income and the amounts you have paid into the fund. There are some exceptions. If you are the spouse of someone who paid in, you may be able to draw on your spouse's retirement benefits, even if you did not work. You may also qualify if you are disabled. Minor children and some disabled adult children may also be entitled to benefits. Minor children of people who are receiving benefits also qualify to receive Social Security. Most states consider the amount the child receives from Social Security as income when calculating child support.

Many people have retirement plans in addition to Social Security. There are two primary forms of retirement plans; the first is the defined-benefit plan. These plans are the traditional pension programs. Railroad and union pensions are examples of defined-benefit plans. The benefit is determined by your top salary for the final few years of work and the total number of years you worked for the company.

The second type is the defined contribution plan. These plans include 401(k) plans, 403(b) plans, and Thrift Savings Plans. In these plans, employees contribute up to 20 percent of their gross income into their retirement fund, and employers match that amount. Once the beneficiary reaches retirement age, they begin drawing from the fund. To encourage retirement savings, the government offers tax incentives for saving for the future and penalizes beneficiaries for withdrawing the funds early. Individual retirement accounts (IRAs) also fall into this category. In general, contributions you made before the marriage remain your property, while any contributions or increases during the marriage are divided equally. For a complete discussion, see chapter 17.

Spouses in long-term marriages often have substantial equity in their homes. In fact, their home may be their single most valuable asset. If you purchased your home early in the marriage, it might be paid off, or nearly so, and you probably have a relatively low house payment, making selling the home the last thing either of you may want to do. But how do you live separately, and which spouse continues to live in the family home? These are questions that will be different for every couple. Does one spouse have more income than the other? If so, perhaps they are the spouse who can best afford to remain in the home. Conversely, could the higher-earning spouse pay spousal support to the lower-earning spouse so they can stay in the house?

Like all divorces, the senior divorce requires thoughtfulness and planning. You must look forward and try to anticipate the future. Writers say there are two kinds of authors: there are those who write by the seat of their pants, furiously getting it all down on paper so they can edit later, and those called plotters, who outline and map every chapter. All people tend to be pantsers or plotters, or like my story from chapter 9, tennis shoes or Tahiti. No matter your age, if you are a pantser, now is not the time to dig your heels in and insist that's how you'll approach your divorce. It's the wrong time to wing it. Instead, force yourself out of your comfort zone and plot and plan a bit; you'll be glad later that you did.

Typically, life insurance, estate planning, and wills and trusts are already a part of a senior couple's financial plan, and unwinding them can be complicated. With many retirement plans, the retiree can take a reduced monthly annuity in return for continuing to receive benefits for their surviving spouse after the member spouse's death. These survivor benefits can be an expensive form of life insurance. Many financial advisors recommend that their clients draw the full amount of the retirement pay and replace the survivor benefits with a life insurance policy at a lower cost.

As an example, I had a client whose husband retired from a career in government. There was a substantial life insurance policy with the wife as beneficiary intended to replace the husband's pension survivor benefits if her husband died before she did. For this client, it was critical to ensure that the life insurance policy remained in full force after the parties' divorce. Without it, the wife was only entitled to nominal Social Security, which would not have been enough for her to live on. The divorce settlement we negotiated required the husband to continue to pay the life insurance premiums and to declare the wife's beneficiary designation irrevocable. That meant the husband couldn't drop the policy or make someone else the beneficiary. It was especially important since the husband had moved on to a new relationship. There are some tricky aspects to this, and you must do it carefully. A life insurance policy is a contract between the spouses and the company. It's crucial to put everything in the judgment to ensure the insurance company follows the parties' instructions. Along with a copy of the judgment, both spouses should sign a cover letter to the insurance company that gives the company instructions. The final divorce judgment and the letter should outline the following:

- The wife's/husband's designation as the sole beneficiary is irrevocable.
- If the policy owner attempts to change the beneficiary, the company will notify the beneficiary immediately.
- If, after those precautions, the policy owner still manages to change the beneficiary, the beneficiary spouse will have a claim on the policy owner's estate superior to all other claims for the full amount of the policy payout plus any attorney fees required to litigate the matter.

These provisions protect the beneficiary spouse from losing their retirement security because the policy-owning spouse changes their mind or becomes vindictive.

Your home is often your most significant asset, and it's essential to protect your interest in it, too. As an example, I represented a woman who had been married for nearly fifty years. When her husband retired several years before, the couple had used much of their accumulated wealth to buy a property outright, so they would not have a house payment. The property was a small gentleman's farm that the husband took great joy in maintaining. The husband, who had a long history of having affairs, began a relationship with a much younger woman who appeared to be keenly interested in his financial assets. My client, his long-suffering wife, finally reached her limit. My client had health problems and was not able to take care of the property without help. The husband wanted to continue living on the farm. In negotiating the divorce settlement, we needed to protect the wife's interest in the joint real estate. After the divorce, my client moved to a condo in town while the husband remained on the farm.

It's necessary to understand how divorce changes real property ownership to tell the rest of this story. In most states, a couple owns a home purchased jointly as "tenants in the entirety," which means both parties hold a 100 percent interest in the property, and if one dies, the other still owns 100 percent of the property. In that situation, neither spouse can give or sell their interest to a third party. When spouses divorce, if they both retain ownership of the real property, they become "tenants in common," which means each of them owns 50 percent interest in the property, and so each could sell, leave in a will, or deed their interest in the property to a third party.

To protect my client's interest in the farm from the husband's gold-digging girlfriend, we insisted on some critical provisions in the judgment. First, we required that the husband execute a will that left all interest in the property and its equipment and stock to the wife. We made sure to list the specific property, including a relatively new tractor, some farm vehicles, an expensive horse with its equally expensive tack, and several head of cattle. We made sure the husband was required to notify the wife if he wrote a new will or made changes to the existing will and that the agreement about the house would remain in all his subsequent wills. We also made sure that if he changed his will, the wife would have a claim against her husband's estate, superior to all other claims for the property's value at the time of the husband's death, plus all her attorney fees. Second, we established the property's current value at the time of the divorce and included it in the divorce judgment as a finding of fact. We made sure both the divorce judgment and the husband's new will were executed and filed with the court.

Finally, we insisted on a provision that stated that if the husband decided to sell the farm, the wife would have the right to buy the property from the husband for the value at the time of the divorce. Yes, these terms were favorable to the wife. Still, had we gone to court, I would have argued to the judge that the terms were reasonable considering their lengthy marriage, the spouses' ages, and relative disparity in their incomes. The husband had retired from a lucrative job. The wife had been a homemaker most of their married life, only working occasional short-term and part-time jobs.

As it turned out, these terms were critical to the wife's future security. Shortly after the divorce, the husband moved the new woman in with him on the farm. For the next two years, the husband and the girlfriend lived on the farm, and the husband continued to pay spousal support to the wife from his substantial retirement income. When the husband died suddenly of a heart attack, the girlfriend was shocked to learn that the farm's ownership reverted solely to the wife. Spousal support obligations end when one partner dies, but, as we intended, the wife sold the farm and invested the proceeds into an annuity that provided her with income to replace her spousal support.

I offer these examples to illustrate how complex this planning can be and to emphasize that you should not leave things to chance. I recommend that you find a knowledgeable lawyer and a good financial advisor to help you.

In most states, couples have the option of legal separation rather than divorce. The pros and cons of each are outlined fully in chapter 6. The reasons to choose separation over divorce can be significant in gray marriages. The most compelling reasons to select separation rather than divorce are medical needs and health insurance. In some cases, spouses choose to remain legally married because one spouse needs and can't obtain medical insurance or when a spouse is incapacitated.

Some health insurance companies have tightened their rules to protect their bottom lines, so check with your provider if you are considering legal separation rather than divorce. I represented a man whose wife had sustained a severe traumatic brain injury in an accident. As is sometimes the case, the injury had caused a drastic personality change in the wife. Even though their relationship had changed radically, when the wife filed for divorce, the husband resisted. The husband didn't want to divorce his wife because he wanted to be available and to have the legal authority to help her if she needed it. In her diminished capacity, it was hard for her to understand that her husband's insurance covered her ongoing medical needs, including additional support and caregivers because of her disabilities. We were able to enlist the wife's attorney to convince her that a legal separation was in her best interest. As long as neither partner was interested in remarrying, the separation was a good option for both spouses.

It's heart wrenching when a spouse becomes physically or mentally incapacitated. Even though you are legally married, you may still not be permitted to make decisions for your incapacitated spouse in some states. Hopefully, you and your spouse executed powers of attorney while you were both still able. If not, you or another family member might have to file for guardianship. Whether to divorce an incapacitated spouse is a personal decision. There may be legal and financial reasons that make divorce advisable. Often, the incapacitated spouse has better access to state and federal disability services if the agency doesn't consider the former spouse's income and assets when evaluating eligibility.

The legal nuances of divorcing someone who is incapacitated are tricky. When you serve a legal document to someone, it's intended to notify that person that a lawsuit has been filed against them so they can defend themselves in court. For service to be effective, the person receiving the documents must understand what they receive. An incapacitated person can't receive or accept the service of legal documents, so they need a guardian who can be served legal papers. To be appointed as guardian, you must file a petition with the court; the court must approve the guardianship and issue an order appointing you. That takes time. If you intend to initiate divorce proceedings, you can't also serve as your spouse's guardian. It's a clear conflict since you have a duty to yourself and a fiduciary duty as a guardian to act in your spouse's best interest. Under these circumstances, your spouse's guardian must be someone other than you. If a family member is not available, there are people you can hire to act as your spouse's guardian. Be advised, however, if a guardian is appointed for your spouse, that person will make all your spouse's medical and financial decisions.

Until now, we've addressed the divorce of seniors only in financial terms, but all divorces take an emotional toll on families. If you have adult children and grandchildren, you may think your divorce will have less impact on them, but adult children of divorcing parents suffer, too. They still worry about how your divorce will affect their relationship with you and the other parent. They still must abandon some of their expectations around family relationships, events, and gatherings. The adult children often become the ones running interference for one or both of you. They wonder how your divorce will affect their children; they worry about who will take care of each of you if it becomes necessary. If the family owns and operates a business, they also worry about succession in the company and how a division of the marital interest in the company affects their income and earnings. As you think and plan for your divorce, remember that families are systems. You will need to be sensitive to the needs and emotions of your adult children as well. If your divorce is acrimonious, things like holidays can become stressful to your children. They may also be managing the families of their spouses on holidays and other family events. Being sensitive to these changes and flexible as you move forward is key to making things a little easier on everyone. A single decision can cascade into many consequences, and the more established the family, the harder those consequences may land.

12

THE GAY MARRIAGE

In June 2015, the U.S. Supreme Court ruled that state bans on same-sex marriages were unconstitutional. The ruling came after forty-five years of activism and visibility following the Stonewall riots in 1969. The path to that landmark ruling in 2015 is strewn with starts, stops, and odd compromises.

Some states introduced civil unions in an attempt to appease activists and critics. Others applied their existing laws about domestic partnerships to same-sex couples. Civil unions became an interim step toward marriage equality, but a civil union is not a marriage, and so these didn't come with that same bundle of rights we've talked about. Unlike a marriage, civil unions were not universally recognized between states. Since civil unions were a construct of each state, a civil union could only give the couple rights within the state that solemnized it. A civil union did not bestow federal rights and benefits on the couple. For example, partners in a civil union could not file joint federal income taxes or receive Social Security survivor and spousal benefits. Once marriage became possible for them, many couples formalized these relationships by marrying.

The method of dissolving a civil union is different from ending a marriage, and the process varies from state to state. In general, you do not have to dissolve your civil union to marry your partner. If you want to marry someone other than your civil union partner, you must dissolve the civil union first.

Before states began recognizing civil unions, the legal concept called domestic partnership arose from the palimony suits of the 1970s. By the 1970s, most states had abandoned the concept of common-law marriage and adopted "no-fault" divorce laws. Historically, common-law marriage was a status conveyed on opposite-sex couples who had lived together as husband and wife and held themselves out as married. The recognition of common-law marriage harkened back to the time in history when the formalities of marriage, such as a license from the state and an officiant to solemnize, were not always available in far-flung rural areas. Only Colorado, Iowa, Kansas, Montana, New Hampshire, Oklahoma, Rhode Island, Texas, the District of Columbia, and Utah still recognize common-law marriages. New Hampshire only recognizes common-law marriage in the context of inheritance. The social upheaval of the 1960s and 1970s led many heterosexual couples to turn their back on traditional social constructs, including marriage. Later, many of those same couples discovered that their rebellion came at a cost. In an early and well-known case, Michelle Triola Marvin sued actor Lee Marvin for alimony, even though the couple had never married. California's courts declined to afford Michelle Triola the same protection for her living arrangement as married couples. In some states, the law governing the dissolution of these informal domestic partnerships is the same as dissolving a business partnership. Since families aren't businesses, that led to some odd results.

When some states developed formal procedures to recognize same-sex unions, they further confused matters by calling them "domestic partnerships" rather than civil unions. In some of those states, the same statutes applied whether you were dissolving a marriage or a domestic partnership. In others, the legislature developed a specific process for dissolution. It's important to point out here that some employers now offer benefits to "domestic partners." Those employers may have their own definition of what constitutes a domestic partner, which may not require any legal recognition.

Since the legalization of same-sex marriages in 2015, most states have done away with civil unions and formalized domestic partnerships. Some states permitted couples that were in civil unions or formalized domestic partnerships to convert them to marriages. Others, such as Connecticut, automatically converted all civil unions to marriages, while other states required couples to obtain a marriage license and go through a marriage ceremony. As of 2015, all marriages, both opposite-sex and same-sex, are solemnized and dissolved under the same state laws.

The laws that apply to property division, support, and debt allocation apply equally to opposite-sex and same-sex couples. The chapters in this book that deal with those issues are equally applicable. Couples that are not legally married but are still relying on their state's version of a civil union or domestic partnership will find the rules different in their states. It will be essential for them to consult with an attorney who specializes in unwinding those legal relationships.

THE GAY MARRIAGE, PARENTHOOD, AND CHILD CUSTODY

Family law isn't always applied equally for same-sex couples in parenthood, child custody, and parenting time. Same-sex couples must use some form of assisted reproduction to become parents, such as donated eggs, sperm, or the employment of surrogates.

The law seldom keeps up with technology, and nowhere is the gap more apparent than in the area of reproductive law. For example, in 1973, when *Roe v. Wade*[1] made abortion legal, the U.S. Supreme court identified a three-trimester scheme. Using the science of the time, the court determined that in the woman's first and second trimesters of pregnancy, the fetus was not viable outside the womb, and therefore the decision to end the pregnancy was solely the mother's. As technology has developed, the point of viability has become a moving target. Under the court's definition, a fetus was not considered viable until the twenty-eighth week of pregnancy. Four decades later, babies as early as twenty-one weeks are surviving with neonatal intensive care intervention. Similar issues arise with assisted reproduction.

One of the most common forms of assisted reproduction, the use of donated sperm, has become a complicated snarl. Most states have laws that protect donor privacy by prohibiting medical providers from ever identifying them. The laws also rule that the sperm donor has no parental rights or responsibilities and that the gestational parent and spouse are the child's legal parents. The rise in popularity of home DNA testing and the databases they have created are blowing the lid off that confidentiality.

Individual clinics may have policies about how often they use a donor's sperm, but the industry is entirely unregulated. While clinics may tell couples that they used sperm from donors in other parts of the country and limit the number of confirmed pregnancies to lessen the chances that half siblings will unwittingly meet and marry, there is no way to control where and when donors donate. Now, thanks to those readily available DNA test kits, young people are discovering they have dozens or even hundreds of half siblings. A single sibling listing their DNA profile in a database can cause an unanticipated cascade of revelations. Medical providers, state legislatures, and parents could not have foreseen the development of home DNA testing when state legislators passed laws that protected anonymous sperm donors and their privacy. Author Dani Shapiro has written a moving memoir about her own experience as a child conceived with donor sperm, called *Inheritance: A Memoir of Genealogy, Paternity, and Love*. During her life, Shapiro questions why she doesn't look like her Jewish family. A commercial DNA test reveals the answer: her parents used donor sperm to achieve pregnancy. With both parents deceased, Shapiro must come to terms with new additions and a reshuffling of her family constellation.

The use of gestational carriers (and surrogate parents) has also become more common. A gestational carrier is a person who agrees to carry a child who is not biologically related to her. An embryo created using the sperm and egg of the parents is implanted in the gestational carrier who carries the baby to term. Surrogate parents are inseminated with the father's sperm and are therefore genetically related to the child. The most notorious surrogate case occurred in 1986 when Mary Beth Whitehead entered into a surrogate contract with a couple, was inseminated with the husband's sperm, and then refused to give the baby up to the biological father and his wife. In a contorted bit of reasoning, the court in New Jersey ruled that surrogate contracts were illegal and invalid but then found that it was in the child's best interest that custody of the baby be awarded to the biological father and his wife. Since that time, states have differed in their recognition of surrogacy. For example, a couple in Michigan, which has an old anti-surrogacy law on the books, was denied a pre-birth determination of custody of their twins. The babies were conceived using only their parents' genetic material and had no genetic relation to their carrier. Despite that, the court ruled that the biological parents must legally adopt the children. The gestational carrier and her husband were listed on the birth certificates, even over their objection. Unwinding these arrangements when parents divorce can be equally complicated. While the above examples arose in the context of cisgender couples, the legal issues remain the same.

Assisted reproduction has become more affordable and widespread, leading to more opportunities to become parents. Childless couples can now "adopt" embryos. When a couple uses in vitro technology, the lab creates many embryos to ensure the couple's chance of success. Often, the genetic parents are unable to use all their embryos. Rather than destroy those embryos, there is a move to make them available for adoption by other hopeful and less fortunate couples. The embryos are either sold or donated to the adoptive parents. The adopted embryo is implanted into the adoptive gestational parent. The child becomes the adoptive parents' legal child, even though the child has no biological relation to those parents. Again, legal questions arise; if couples pay for the embryos, does it violate laws against baby selling? Since the embryo is the donor couple's genetic child, must the new parents legally adopt their own child? With assisted reproduction options ever expanding, more and more couples will inevitably find themselves in this legal quagmire.

Pouring the emotional accelerant of divorce onto an already complicated parenting situation is the perfect setup for a litigation bonfire I like to call "who's your daddy?" Remember that **Rule 1** applies whether you are a same-sex or opposite-sex couple: *Whatever this shit is, it belongs to you. Don't make your shit your children's shit. Ever.*

If you and your same-sex spouse have children, expect your lawyer to ask some direct and detailed personal questions about exactly how you got these children, who they are genetically, and precisely who is on their birth certificates. That's because the answers can have ramifications on custody and parenting time, and it's another area where the law hasn't kept up with technological and social changes. In many ways, the law still views birth certificates like car titles. Whose name is on the title—oops—birth certificate? In a few more progressive states, both parents can be listed on the child's birth certificate, even if they are the same gender. In many, less progressive—dare I say backward?—states, the birth certificate must follow genetics. The father's name may be left off a birth certificate, but an additional mother may not be added. In other words, if you are in a lesbian marriage where one parent becomes pregnant with the help of donor sperm, the birth parent may be the only one listed on the birth certificate. Some states permit the nonbiological parent to adopt the child in a process known as a stepparent adoption. If the nonbiological parent has done so, the law treats the child as if they were born to both parents naturally, even when it's a physical impossibility.

While societal definitions are becoming more elastic, the legal definitions are lagging. Consider a transgender person who identifies as male but is still physically female and becomes pregnant. While he will likely identify in his family as the child's father, where does his name appear on the birth certificate? For purposes of the birth certificate, is he the child's mother? And what about his wife? Where does she appear in the legal documents? It's more than just an intellectual exercise because we are talking about how parents' identity defines their rights and responsibilities.

Many families, both gay and cisgender, adopt children. Children adopted during a marriage are legally the adoptive parents' children as if they had been born to them. Some states allow unmarried partners to adopt children, and some do not. A complication may come if the children are legally adopted by one partner but not the other. If you are a divorcing gay parent with children conceived using alternative reproductive technologies or have a child adopted by only one partner, you should consult right away with a lawyer specializing in Rainbow law and who can help you navigate the uncertainty.

Here's the thing: no matter how you got that child, and whether you are cisgender or LGBTQ, your child needs the same thing from you: love, support, and the sense of security that comes from knowing they can always count on you, no matter what. Getting divorced doesn't relieve you of that responsibility, even momentarily.

13

THE MILITARY MARRIAGE

If you are retired from the military or currently serving, thank you. There is nothing that renews my faith more than knowing there are still people willing to put their lives on the line for something they believe in. The military has its own language, and thanks to the twenty years I spent in the U.S. Air Force and Air National Guard, it's a language I speak.

All military family members serve, whether you are the military member, the civilian spouse, or the children waiting at home. Without question, military culture is different and, to the uninitiated, mystifying. The Vietnam War occurred while I was growing up, and because there was still a draft, most people knew someone who had served or was serving. People were more conversant with military rules, customs, and traditions. Today, less than 1 percent of the population serves in the military, making most of us oblivious to military families' challenges. Military divorces can be complicated.

Change comes slowly to military culture. When I first joined, military spouses had far less freedom, far less support, and far fewer opportunities. There was a time that when a military member received a performance evaluation their superior would ask, "How much volunteer service does your spouse do?" The military expected spouses to put their education and career pursuits on hold to support and follow their spouses. Even though modern military families are more egalitarian, there's no question that military membership still requires sacrifice. Deployments and battle trauma take their toll on families. When a spouse deploys, their day-to-day role in the family shrinks. When a deployed spouse comes home, they might feel there is no room left for them in their family. Even when the military focuses on assuring returning members have a "soft landing," friction and confusion are inevitable. Despite the hardships, the rate of divorce in the military is roughly the same as in civilian populations.

Interestingly, according to the website Military.com, divorce rates for female service members are nearly triple that of their male counterparts.[1] Women also leave military service at higher rates than their male counterparts. From my personal experience, I think this happens because a warrior's societal expectations are very different from those of a wife, and sometimes, one or the other has to give.

LOSING BENEFITS

Civilian spouses of military members stand to lose a great deal in divorce, even if the actual divorce settlement appears fair. About one-third of military families live in subsidized housing on military installations. When couples divorce, the nonmember spouse loses the benefit and must move from military housing within thirty days. The nonmember also loses their TRICARE health insurance coverage. If the couple has been married for at least fifteen years, the nonmember spouse can receive a year of transitional medical benefits, after which they may buy continued coverage for up to thirty-six months. Those married less than fifteen years don't receive transitional coverage but may buy continued TRICARE coverage for up to thirty-six months through the Continued Health Care Benefit Program (CHCBP). CHCBP is the military version of the federal Consolidated Omnibus Budget Reconciliation Act (COBRA), the federal law that allows divorcing spouses to buy a continuation of their health benefits through their spouse's employment. Compared to most civilian COBRA plans, the CHCBP benefits are a good deal, and I always advise clients to enroll. If the nonmember spouse allows their CHCBP coverage to lapse before the end of the thirty-six months, it can't be reinstated.

The military member's biological and adopted children, from birth to age twenty-one (or age twenty-three if they are students), remain covered by TRICARE. Children over the age of twenty-three may enroll in the TRICARE Young Adult plan until age twenty-six if they don't have coverage available through an employer. The TRICARE

Young Adult (TYA) program is premium based, but again, in comparison with civilian plans, it is quite affordable.

Parents must ensure the children have and maintain current military dependent ID cards because it also retains their enrollment in DEERS, the Defense Enrollment Eligibility Reporting System. Allowing the children's ID to expire can cause a lapse in health coverage. The custodial parent must also notify military officials immediately of any address change for the children. Usually, the military member must accompany the child and complete paperwork, so getting a new ID card may require the military member spouse's cooperation. There are procedures for renewing a child's ID card if the member spouse is deployed.

CUSTODY AND PARENTING TIME

Military members face unique challenges around custody and parenting time. Single military members who have sole custody of their children must make provisions for what happens in the event of their death or capture or if they receive orders for an extended deployment. Typically, the noncustodial parent is designated as the children's alternate custodian. However, if the noncustodial parent is not suitable or is unavailable, you will be required to designate someone to care for the children when you are unavailable or unable. Out of necessity, parenting-time schedules must be flexible so that the children can maintain a good relationship with their military parent, despite deployments, moves, and other service-related absences.

One advantage of having a military former spouse is that military rules are strict. Military commanders do not take it lightly when a person under their command doesn't pay their support. Often, a single call to a soldier, sailor, or airman's commander or first sergeant is sufficient to solve the problem of delinquent support payments.

RETIREMENT AND DISABILITY BENEFITS

The division of military retirement benefits is often the most complex part of a military divorce. Military retirement benefits are a defined-benefit plan. For additional explanations about retirement plans, see chapter 17. Like other types of defined-benefit plans, the amount a military retiree receives when they retire is based on the member's rank and their years of service at the time of retirement. Military retirements are divided between spouses, but those retirement benefits don't vest until the military member becomes eligible to retire. If a military member leaves the service before they have served for twenty years, no retirement benefits are paid. Those who retire from active service can begin drawing their retirement payments as soon as they retire. Members of the National Guard and the Reserves are also entitled to retirement pay after twenty years of creditable service but are not eligible to begin drawing their retirement pay until they reach age sixty.

Let me give you some illustrations. Say Jessica has been on active duty in the U.S. Air Force for thirteen years. She and her husband, Greg, have two children. Greg is not in the service. When Jessica and Greg divorce, Jessica is awarded custody of their children. Jessica must complete paperwork giving Greg temporary custody of the children if Jessica is deployed, captured, or killed. Jessica can continue to live in the housing complex on the base with the children, but Greg will have to move out. Jessica will continue to receive housing and dependent allowances for the children but not for Greg. Greg will be able to buy continuing medical coverage for up to thirty-six months through TRICARE. Jessica's retirement fund can be split between her and Greg, but neither will receive anything from that retirement unless Jessica completes twenty years of service. The retirement may be divided according to what the parties agree, but in general, the benefits are split equally for any years of service that occurred during their marriage. Once a judge signs their divorce judgment, Jessica and Greg will hire a lawyer specializing in military retirements to draft a Qualified Domestic Relations Order (QDRO) directing the military retirement system on how to divide Jessica's future pension. Since Jessica will be serving at least seven more years, it's reasonable for them to divide only the value of the thirteen years Jessica has already served but not the future seven years. Once Jessica reaches the twenty-year service mark, Greg may begin drawing his portion, even if Jessica doesn't retire. Since the parties were married for more than ten years, Greg can opt to have his payments sent directly to him from the government.

Military retirement pay and disability payments made by the U.S. Department of Veterans Affairs (VA) are different but are often confused. The benefits are paid by different agencies and under different circumstances and with varying requirements of eligibility. The VA grants disabled veterans benefits regardless of their years of service. A veteran's medical status is assessed, and the amount of their benefit is determined based on the severity and the duration of their disability, expressed as a percentage. Veteran benefits are not taxable, while military retirement payments are treated as ordinary income. A military member with twenty years of satisfactory service receives a pension. The amount is set based on their rank and years of service. If that person also has a service-connected disability, they may also receive benefits from the VA. Under the Concurrent Retirement and Disability Payments (CRDP) rules, if the veteran is rated by the VA as less than 50 percent disabled, any compensation they receive from the VA will be deducted from their military retirement. The advantage to them is that any VA compensation is received tax free. If the VA classifies the veteran as 50 percent or more disabled, they will receive the total amount of both their military pension and their VA disability benefits.

PARENTING AFTER A MILITARY DIVORCE

Parenting children after divorce is challenging. Parenting children after divorce while in the military may increase that exponentially. As a military member, you're already pulled in many directions. Add in parenting, and the competing interests can pull you in opposite directions. You may be away from your children for long periods or may move frequently. You joined the military to be part of something bigger than you, to create a legacy that lives beyond you. You probably had children for the same reason. Now, you may feel your situation is forcing you to choose one over the other. It is possible to be a responsible service member and a responsible parent, but it takes dedication, planning, and a willingness to accept others' help. Cultivating an appreciative and respectful parenting relationship with your coparent will help you achieve both. We are fortunate that technology makes remaining in contact with children easier. In your grandparents' time, a letter from Vietnam could take a month to arrive, and ridiculously expensive phone calls were difficult to arrange and reserved for special occasions and emergencies. Today, it's possible for parents to see and talk to their children by video conference nearly every day, even from the edge of the battlefield. If your coparent is a military member, their military obligations will require you to make some compromises. You might think that once you're divorced, your sacrifices for your spouse's military career will end. They won't, so let me just thank you now for your continuing service to both our country and your children. As we have discussed before (okay, perhaps belabored a bit), children need both parents, and it's going to take a few heroics on your part to make sure your children have a relationship with their military parent. Sometimes it will suck. Do it anyway. If it means getting up in the middle of the night so your kids can video chat with their deployed parent or recording the recital and sending it to the other parent, do it for your children. If it means rearranging parenting time to accommodate Guard weekends or deal with last-minute TDYs (temporary duty assignments), do it. You must be flexible with scheduling and make your children's time with their military parent a priority when it's scarce and precious.

BATTLE TRAUMA

Military service can cost members far more than they gain. Nowhere is that more evident than with members who have trauma-related conditions. No one knows why battle trauma affects some more than others. Most military members who are in combat situations experience what is called combat stress. The symptoms usually subside once the person is out of the situation. When that trauma becomes chronic, they are diagnosed with posttraumatic stress disorder (PTSD). You may want to review my theory of the pickle jar from chapter 3. The long-term impact of battle trauma can severely impact custody and parenting time. That's not only because of the symptoms but also because of the expectations of family and friends. For example, I had a client whose deployment in the Middle East was cut short when he had a mental health crisis. He returned to the United States and entered a program for returning soldiers. He did well in the treatment program and was later discharged honorably from his military service because of his disability. To his credit, my client faithfully attended his therapy sessions and took his prescribed medications. Even so, his former wife resisted him seeing his young children, claiming that he required supervision because of his mental health condition. We fought hard for a couple of years, and in the end, my client overcame everyone's reservations and has a great relationship with his children as a result.

Twenty-two (22). That's the average number of military members and veterans who commit suicide every day. According to the U.S. Veterans Administration, on average, eighteen veterans and four active, reserve, or guard members take their own lives daily. The number has remained consistent over the past ten years, but there are indications that the pandemic may have contributed to a recent rise.[2] As veterans, it's our responsibility, if we're able, to buddy-check our friends. As the former spouse of a veteran, it's your responsibility, too. The suicide of a parent will have a lifelong impact on a child. Do it for your kids.

If you are a military member suffering from battle trauma, you are not alone. According to the U.S. Department of Veterans Affairs, PTSD affects between 11 percent and 30 percent of battle participants, depending on the conflict. Twenty-three percent of women experience sexual violence and trauma while in the military.[3] It means your service isn't done when you separate because it's your responsibility to find treatment and work at recovery. EMDR (Eye Movement Desensitization and Reprocessing) therapy is particularly helpful in treating trauma. It was your responsibility in battle to keep yourself and your buddies safe; now, it's your responsibility to keep you and your family safe. Recovery is possible.

If you are the spouse or former spouse of a military member with battle trauma, understand that there are resources available for your veteran. Even though you're divorced, it's reasonable for you to expect that your spouse will participate in those services and give the treatment providers permission to verify that they are active in their treatment and taking their prescribed medication. It is not reasonable to expect that the treatment provider will share the substance of your former spouse's treatment.

It's possible to have a military career while coparenting. The skills that you've learned in the military—leadership, organization, and dedication— all translate into good parenting if you apply them. There are many resources to be found online. The following are some websites to check out: U.S. Department of Defense (defense.gov), Military OneSource (militaryonesource.mil), Military.com, and Sandboxx (sandboxx.us).

14

SILLY COURT

Consider this chapter as both a cautionary tale and a palate cleanser. The following examples, while amusing, also serve to emphasize the importance of being honest with your lawyer and reasonable in your expectations. We're about to delve into some of the most complex parts of your divorce in the following chapters, so enjoy this brief interlude.

Sometimes, in the heat of the moment, people make foolish decisions, including insisting on going to court for silly reasons. To avoid wasting time and money on silly court, hire a competent lawyer and take their advice. Don't get me wrong, sometimes going to court is the only way to resolve your dispute with your ex, but save court for when it's really necessary. Sometimes going to court, especially in the early part of a case, can be unnecessary or just plain silly. It can be a waste of time, energy, and money for several reasons. First, the judge may not have the power to give you what you want, and second, you might be asking the wrong way or at the wrong time.

Consider one of my potential clients. The woman came to me, asking me to represent her in a stalking order hearing. She had filed the stalking order against her long-time partner, and he had contested the order and asked for a hearing. Stalking orders are a specific species of protective order. They require that the "stalker" subject the victim to repeated and unwanted contact. Think of the character Joe Goldberg in the novel and Netflix series *You*. Stalking orders keep people like him from lurking outside homes and businesses and following their victims in real life and online.

In this case, my potential client could not articulate a single instance where her boyfriend had actually stalked her. She also couldn't come up with a single time he had abused her or placed her in fear of abuse, which meant there was also no basis for a domestic violence protective order either. His offense? He'd stopped paying her rent several months after he moved out of their shared house and broke off his relationship with her. She was using the stalking order to punish him. Even though I told her repeatedly that she did not have any legal basis for the stalking order and that the judge would undoubtedly dismiss it as baseless, she insisted she wanted a hearing. Now I had a choice to make. Lawyers are expected to represent our clients zealously, but our professional responsibility rules also prevent us from bringing frivolous suits or perpetrating a fraud on the court. This one was a no-brainer. I declined to represent the woman, and she went on to represent herself in court.

I haven't always been able to dodge silly court, and there are times I've wanted to crawl under the counsel table when a client opened their mouth on the stand. There was, for instance, the time I represented a woman in a domestic violence restraining order case. I knew this woman through a volunteer organization that I had some involvement with, and she came to me for help when her former boyfriend contested the restraining order she had filed against him. The hearing was already scheduled when I met with the woman and went over her story in depth. There seemed ample facts to support the restraining order, and when we arrived at the hearing that morning, I was confident that the judge would uphold the protective order. My client got on the witness stand and told her story. She was tearful, fearful, and convincing. The hearing took a radical turn, though, when the boyfriend took the stand. While it's not unusual for parties to tell different stories, this hearing went radically off the rails fast.

The boyfriend reported that the confrontation central to the restraining order had not happened quite how my client had described it in her petition. No, he had not forced his way into the house to retrieve his belongings. No, he had not slammed her against a wall, and yes, he had a witness who had been there with him. The boyfriend said he'd taken the friend because he was worried about what my client might do. The boyfriend pointed out his friend, who was sitting in the courtroom, waving from the gallery and waiting to testify. In fact, he said, my client had pulled a gun (a weapon he knew she kept loaded) from her nightstand and pointed it at him to keep him from taking a box of things out of the closet. The judge, whose curiosity was now piqued, called my client back to the stand. Calling someone back to the stand is something judges can but rarely do. He reminded my client she was under oath and asked her if she had pulled her gun on the boyfriend. She hung her head and nodded. I am sure the judge could tell from the expression on my face that this was new information to me. The judge leaned over toward my client and asked, "What was so important in that box?"

"Toys," my client answered, almost too quiet to hear.

"Toys?"

"You know, adult toys."

The judge dismissed the restraining order and gave my client a stern lecture on abusing the system. I was glad I'd gotten a retainer upfront to cover my fees. It's hearings like this that convinced me I never wanted to be a judge.

Over the years, I've seen motions, most thankfully from the other side of my cases, requesting that the court order some pretty interesting things. Often, these are motions filed early in a divorce case to retrieve property, especially if a person needs the property for work. I've seen a musician who needed his guitars; contractors, plumbers, and electricians who needed their work vans and tools; and a wedding DJ who needed his equipment and his recorded rock 'n' roll. I even received a motion from another attorney seeking to force my client to return his spouse's whips and chains, which she claimed were the tools of her trade as a dominatrix.

The worst of these cases are the ones about money. I can't count the times I've seen one spouse demand impossible amounts of temporary support from the other. Just so you know, it's illegal for a judge to manufacture money.

The other silly cases are where one partner tries to force the other to be a better person. You know, one spouse tries to force the other to see the children or stop making the children see the new partner. A word of caution: the judge doesn't have the power to improve your spouse's character.

A clear understanding of what the law and judges can and can't do and a realistic view of your case's facts are the best ways to avoid wasting your money on silly and unnecessary court hearings.

15

MONEY

Ah, money. To some, the root of all evil, to others, the source of all happiness, but invariably the great divider. Having too little or spending too much causes conflict between couples. Face it: there is nothing more intimate than sharing your financial situation with a partner. For many of us, being open about earning, saving, and spending money feels as vulnerable as being naked. Being honest about money takes trust and personal tolerance for vulnerability. When trust in your relationship breaks down, it breaks down everywhere, and when infidelity creeps in, it creeps in everywhere, including in your spending.

An urban legend claims disagreements about money are the basis of most divorces, but statistics don't bear that out. In my experience, secrecy and infidelity cause most divorces, and infidelity comes in many brands. Sometimes it's romantic or sexual infidelity, but sometimes it's financial infidelity. It's secret accounts or secret spending, sometimes brought on by a secret addiction. In any case, the cause is the secret and the feeling of betrayal when the secret becomes known.

Once a couple decides to divorce, while it would be fair to say they think first about their children, the logistics and financial realities are part of that equation. Where will they live, how will they cope, and how will they pay for the massive life changes that are about to happen? How will they go on once they are financially disentangled from each other?

One of the first things your attorney will do is ask you to give them all of your financial information. Observe **Rule 4**: *Don't lie. Not to your lawyer, not to a judge, and not in court documents* and **Rule 6**: *Don't hide income, property, or debt*. Your lawyer is only as good as the information you give them.

The sample documents in appendix A include a list of information you should be compiling. A reminder, the more of this work you do yourself, the less you have to pay your lawyer to do. For some of my clients, directing their attention to this was a distraction that gave them something to do, while others didn't have the emotional bandwidth left to tackle it. Either way works, as long as your lawyer gets the information. Just know that if you drop a couple of banker's boxes on your lawyer's desk, her assistant will spend hours sorting and organizing your paperwork, and she will bill you for that time. If you take the time to do all the sorting and organizing yourself, you'll save yourself a lot of money.

As **Rule 6** says, you must be brutally honest with your lawyer and disclose all your assets and all your debts. As a rule, property divisions in divorce are final and can't be modified once the final judgment is signed. The one exception is when one partner hides assets from the other. In the state where I practiced, the law imposes consequences if you don't disclose all your assets. If you don't disclose, and it's later discovered, a judge can award the hidden asset to the defrauded spouse. Here's an example of why hiding assets can be dangerous. A physician and his wife divorced after a long marriage; they had substantial assets, and the divorce was acrimonious. After the divorce was final, the wife received a piece of the husband's mail. It was a bill from a boat moorage in a neighboring state. Since the doctor and his wife didn't own a boat, she was understandably curious. She and a friend took a drive to the moorage and discovered a beautiful and very expensive sailboat in the rented slip. The boat had a cute doctor-related name, like *PostOp* or *Doctor's Orders*. The harbormaster confirmed the boat belonged to the ex-husband and had been moored there for a couple of years. The wife's attorney filed a motion to reopen the case, and the judge awarded the valuable boat to the wife.

When you get divorced, two can't live as cheaply as one, and there will be sacrifices. Divorce forces you to prioritize your spending. Maintaining your children will be the court's priority. To do that, judges award child support and perhaps support for your former spouse. States may call that support alimony, spousal support, or separate maintenance. Whatever you call it, most people don't like paying it. Still, let's remember there was a time when you loved that person and when you made many, perhaps improbable, promises to one another. Unwinding those promises will take patience and require that you give each other a bit of grace. It's not easy, I know, amid this anger and grief.

CHILD SUPPORT

The law awards child support according to a relatively straightforward formula established by your state. The calculations consider each parent's income, the amount of time the children spend with each parent, and any extraordinary expenses such as the children's special needs and long-distance travel costs. Child support also considers other income sources such as Social Security or Veteran's benefits received for the child. States vary on when child support terminates. In the majority of states, child support ends when the child reaches adulthood at age eighteen. A handful of states offer some support beyond age eighteen as long as the child is attending school. Some states also allow the continuation of child support beyond age eighteen if the child is permanently disabled. Most states don't require a parent to pay extra for private school, college tuition, or extraordinary expenses such as private lessons, sports equipment, musical instruments, or travel for school or extracurricular activities. Parents must provide health insurance if available through their employment or labor union and share the cost of any uninsured medical expense, including prescriptions and copays. That includes medical, dental, orthodontic, optical, and mental health treatment. The paying spouse may also be required to maintain a life insurance policy to make up for support that won't get paid if they died before their obligation ends. Child support may be awarded per child or aggregated, depending on your state's laws. In general, the award for the first child is more than the award for additional children.

The way child support is collected varies from state to state, but in most states, a state agency assists with collecting child support, and there's a preference in the law for all support to go through that agency. Allowing the state to collect your support means that you don't have to. In most cases, the state will collect the support directly from your former spouse's wages each month and deposit it in your account. If your former spouse works as a private contractor or is self-employed, the paying parent pays the state, and the state disburses the funds. Most states turn support payments around quickly; some even have specific time limits on how long the state has to disburse support, so state involvement should not delay your support by more than two or three working days. All fifty states have adopted the Uniform Interstate Family Support Act (UIFSA). Under that act, states must collect support from their resident even if the support order is from another state. For example, Jenny and Lenny live in Texas, and when they divorce, Lenny is ordered by the Texas court to pay child support. Lenny then moves to California. Jenny can't enforce her Texas support order directly with California, but Texas officials can and will enforce it if she initiates a collection action there.

If a receiving spouse draws state assistance in cash welfare payments, child care subsidies, or food stamps, and they are supposed to be receiving child support, the state can go after the non-paying spouse to repay the state. If a parent obligated to pay loses their job, they may ask for a temporary reduction or suspension of their support obligation until they find a new job.

SPOUSAL SUPPORT / ALIMONY

Unlike child support, there is no formula for calculating spousal support. Instead, the court takes into consideration a list of factors. The most common factors are the following:

- Length of the marriage
- Income and earning capacity
- Education
- Work experience including absence from the workforce to raise children
- Health or disability, including mental health
- Minor children in the home
- Standard of living during the marriage

A spouse in a long-term marriage with minimal education who has never worked outside the home and has health problems will be awarded more support than a college-educated spouse with a good job in a short-term marriage.

One factor that often causes conflict or consternation is the standard of living during the marriage. The law dictates that spouses should receive support to maintain a lifestyle similar to the one they had during the marriage. Remembering that two can never live as cheaply as one, that may be a tall order, and judges regularly struggle with that decision. Thinking about why, let's look at a case. I represented a woman who had been married to her husband for more than twenty years. They had two middle-grade children, and the wife had some extremely serious health problems. The husband was a highly educated professional with a lucrative job. The wife, while educated herself, had been absent from her career for many years, first to raise the couple's children and later because of her health. While I've found most spouses try to be fair, this particular man was adamant that since he had earned all the assets, it was all his money, and once the divorce was final, he wanted nothing more to do with the wife. It was clear to everyone that he wanted his life to be as if the wife had never existed. If the judge had not applied the law and ordered the husband to provide support for the wife, the consequences to her could have been catastrophic. The judge ordered that the husband pay spousal support that allowed the wife to maintain her lifestyle and care for her children. I'm pleased to say that the wife's health improved over time, and she was able to resume her career slowly and on a limited basis. That might not have been possible if the judge had not ordered the husband to pay support.

In many states, spousal support is categorized based on the reason for the award. The three categories are transitional, maintenance, and compensatory, and how support is categorized is important.

- **Transitional** support is awarded to a spouse to aid their transition from marriage to single life. That often includes support for some time to allow a spouse to further their education or permit them to be home with children until they are school age.
- **Maintenance** support is awarded for long-term marriages where there is little chance that the lower-income spouse will ever catch up in earning capacity.

- **Compensatory** support is awarded to compensate a spouse for their contribution to the other spouse's earning capacity.

Some states require that the final divorce judgment specify the type of support. Even if your state does not require it, it's still a good idea. It's vital that your judgment spell out the category of support, the reason the support was awarded, and the factors applied in reaching that amount because the conditions at the time of the divorce are the starting point in any future modification. Without that, a later modification will be difficult and could lead to an unfair outcome. See chapter 20 for more on modifying spousal support.

If your case goes to trial, the judge will consider income, assets, and debts, including taxes. Most states define income the same way the Internal Revenue Service does: any money paid to you from any source. The money you receive for your work is income, but so is rent on property you own, bonuses, investment income, pensions, Social Security and Veterans Administration benefits, gifts, contest or gambling winnings, and royalties. The money you inherit from someone else is not income, but if you receive an annual gift from a living parent, an annuity, or other payment from a trust, those are income. If you work in an industry where your work is seasonal, you are expected to put away money during the good season to pay support in the off-season. If you lose your job, you may be able to ask for a temporary suspension or reduction of your child or spousal support payments. Unemployment benefits are considered income.

PROFESSIONAL DEGREES / INCREASED EARNING POTENTIAL

Depending on the state, a professional degree may be considered income or viewed as property. In all states, a spouse must have earned the degree during the marriage. This situation arises when one spouse works during the early marriage to put their partner through school. Then the better-educated spouse goes on to have increased earning capacity. If you are awarded more support or support for a longer duration because of your spouse's increased earning capacity, your final divorce judgment must include the reason for the higher support. Both child and spousal support are nearly always modifiable if there is a substantial change in either former spouse's circumstances. To ensure you don't lose any support that was awarded to compensate for your partner's degree, the reasons the support was awarded must appear in writing in the final judgment.

INHERITANCES

Inheritances are not considered income or a marital asset unless you have comingled them in joint marital accounts. As long as the inherited money has been kept separate, it's the property of the person who inherited it.

PENDING LAWSUITS

There are occasions where divorcing spouses are involved in lawsuits at the time of divorce. The individual circumstances and the reason for the suit will have something to do with how those lawsuit proceeds might be divided. For example, if the lawsuit arose from an auto accident where both spouses were in the car, and both are plaintiffs in the case, they should share in any award. Likewise, proceeds from a lawsuit against a contractor for negligent work on the jointly owned family home should be shared. If, on the other hand, the suit is the result of sexual harassment at work during the marriage, the harassed employee's spouse might not have a claim to any settlement their spouse might receive. The situation where a spouse is injured to the point of disability on the job might be a bit more complicated. It's best to consult a lawyer if either partner is involved in a lawsuit at the time of the divorce.

HEALTH INSURANCE

When you divorce, your children can remain on your spouse's health insurance, but you can't. If you don't have health insurance available through your employer, there are some options. There is a federal law called the Consolidated Omnibus Reconciliation Act (COBRA) covering health care for divorcing spouses. Under that law, you may continue your health insurance with your spouse's employer for up to eighteen months after your divorce is final if you pay the premium. COBRA premiums tend to be expensive, and there may be other options. Be sure to research alternatives such as state-sponsored group plans and other Obamacare options before committing to COBRA benefits. You must decide within thirty days whether you want COBRA benefits, and if you decline them, you can't go back and get them later.

Many employers offer Health Savings Accounts (HSA) as a benefit of employment. HSAs are funds that you contribute to pre-tax and can draw on to pay out-of-pocket medical expenses. If you or your spouse has one of these accounts, it should be divided equally. Be advised, though, that there are restrictions on how the funds can be spent and by whom. You may also want to propose that the spouse with the HSA bear more responsibility for the children's future out-of-pocket medical expenses.

DEBTS

Divorces don't just divide income and property; they also allocate debt. Most families have debt, and some have more debt than they should. Just like income and assets, divorcing spouses must share the marital debt. The reality is that judges are most likely to assign the responsibility to pay a debt to the person who can most afford to pay it. The obligation to pay a debt is a contract between you and the lender. The court doesn't have any authority to remake that contract just because you are divorcing. For instance, the judge can't remove your name from the home mortgage; only your lender can do that. Most lenders require a complete refinance to remove one spouse from a mortgage, and it can be tricky qualifying for the mortgage on only one income. Likewise, credit card companies will only release your spouse's name from an account if the balance is zero. Once you've paid it off, the company will simply close the joint account and reopen an account in your name.

If your debts exceed your income following divorce, it may be tempting to declare bankruptcy. If you are considering bankruptcy, it's essential to consult a lawyer who specializes in those cases. Federal law governs bankruptcy, and like all federal law, it's made by bureaucrats who have nothing better to do than tinker with the rules. A good bankruptcy attorney stays current on all the inevitable changes. Once a person files for bankruptcy, a person called a trustee manages the case and decides who gets paid and in what order from the bankrupt's assets. Spousal and child support are not dischargeable in bankruptcy, and bankruptcy only relieves the person filing for bankruptcy from a debt. That means if the judge ordered your former spouse to pay the joint Visa bill, and instead, they declare bankruptcy, Visa can still come after you. That's right, the debt is still your responsibility because you were a joint holder on the account, so if your former spouse might declare bankruptcy, it's essential to protect yourself. One way to do that is to have your former spouse pay spousal support to you to pay the debts. Another is to put specific language in your divorce judgment that says, "Husband will pay $_____ per month spousal support. As additional spousal support (or in lieu of spousal support), Husband will pay the joint marital obligations to [list the creditors] until paid in full." If the debt payment is considered a form of spousal support, the obligation *might* survive bankruptcy. I say *might* because it's still up to the bankruptcy trustee to decide whether it's a form of spousal support or if it's just a ploy to avoid the non-bankrupting spouse having to pay the debt. If it appears that there is so much marital debt that the only choice is to wipe the slate clean for both of you, declaring bankruptcy jointly could be the best choice. If you declare bankruptcy together, it will slow the divorce process considerably. Bankruptcy will also degrade your credit for seven to ten years and make buying a home, a car, or getting a credit card difficult after your divorce.

Student loans are not generally dischargeable in bankruptcy, although there are a few narrow exceptions. The federal government backs student loans, and while the feds don't care if your debts to Visa or the electric company get written off, they don't take kindly to losing money on student loans. Here's another bit of bad news. Remember how we talked about professional degrees being a joint asset if one spouse helped the other get that degree? Well, the student loans for that degree could also be considered joint debt. These days, student loans associated with law school or medical school can easily top six figures. If you share in the benefit of your spouse's advanced degree, a judge may also make you responsible for part of the debt that funded that degree.

Bank accounts, retirement accounts, and investments are considered property and are covered in chapter 17.

PRENUPTIAL AGREEMENTS

Couples sometimes sign a prenuptial agreement. There have been books written about prenuptial agreements' pros and cons; this isn't one of them. This book is about what to do if you already signed one.

An enforceable prenuptial agreement must have several things. First, it must have a complete inventory of all the assets and liabilities of both parties, including values at the time of the signing. Second, it must clearly document that the parties had time to fully consider the agreement and consult with their separate attorneys about it. Third, it should have been signed well in advance of the wedding so neither party can claim later they were pressured into signing just days or moments before the wedding. The agreement should contain specifics about when and under what circumstances the parties signed the agreement.

Prenuptial agreements can limit spousal support but can't limit child support. Courts have consistently ruled any agreement that limits child support is against public policy because it could force children onto welfare. I once had a client who had entered into a prenuptial agreement that said the parties had decided not to have children together. The husband was quite a bit older than the wife and was wealthy. Their agreement went on to say if the wife became pregnant, she would be solely responsible for the upkeep, care, and raising of the child, and the husband would not be obligated to pay child support. Of course, the woman did become pregnant, and the husband promptly filed for divorce and cited the prenuptial agreement in refusing to pay child support. We asked the court to make a preliminary ruling on the enforceability of the prenuptial agreement. The judge quickly and summarily told the husband the prenuptial agreement was unenforceable. In a twist, instead of just invalidating the section of the prenuptial agreement that dealt with child support, the judge found the whole deal was an unconscionable contract (meaning it was unfair and likely obtained under duress) and threw the entire thing out. That ruling paved the way for my client to ask not only for child support but also for spousal support. Lest you think this was an unfair outcome for the husband, consider that the parties had been married for about ten years. They had followed the husband worldwide, supporting him as he built a successful international business.

The moral of the story is that prenuptial agreements can be, and regularly are, successfully challenged in court during divorce proceedings. To be honest, most judges don't like them. If you find a judge who does, it's probably because he's bitter about his own divorce. If you have a prenuptial agreement, don't assume the game is over. Talk to your attorney about it, and be sure to explain the circumstances at the time you signed the agreement.

POSTNUPTIAL AGREEMENTS

Couples sometimes sign what is called a postnuptial agreement. These are agreements signed after the marriage and are intended to revise the legal relationship after the wedding. There are several reasons these agreements are questionable. First, they monkey around with the bundle of rights every married couple gets. There's a long-standing legal concept of marital unity that says a husband and wife can't contract with one another. Also, a postnuptial agreement can interfere with the fiduciary duty one partner owes to the other. Second, the agreement may not be enforceable as a contract. Basic contract law requires that two people negotiate an agreement at arm's length and that the agreement include an offer, the acceptance of the offer, and some sort of compensation. The compensation (what the law calls consideration) does not have to be money. In a prenuptial agreement, the consideration is the marriage. In a postnuptial agreement, the marriage has already taken place. Sometimes couples enter into a postnuptial agreement after they separate and then reconcile. In that case, the consideration is continuing the marriage. Sometimes one partner demands a postnuptial agreement because their situation has changed, maybe because they won the lottery or invented something like sticky notes (because what did we do before sticky notes?). In the second instance, courts often find the agreements unconscionable and therefore unenforceable.

16

PROPERTY

Stuff. Why are we so attached to it? Why do we think our stuff is so much better and more valuable than everyone else's stuff? Psychologists tell us it's because we see our stuff as an extension of ourselves. I guarantee that the first time your lawyer says, "it's just stuff," you are going to lose your mind. I have theories about a lot of things, and stuff is no exception. Divorce is a traumatic loss. No one likes loss because it makes us feel powerless. Keeping the stuff, especially if it's something your spouse loves, feels like you're taking some of that power back. Sure, it's only stuff, but it's your stuff, and choosing what to do with it makes you feel like you have control over something.

The law puts our stuff into two basic categories: real property and personal property. Real property is real estate. To the layperson, it sounds odd. "After all," you might say, "isn't my TV just as real as my house?" The answer is yes, but someone back in the annals of time and British common law decided that's how we would classify property. Rest assured, your TV is not just a figment of your imagination.

Most states divide property using what is called the common law or the equitable division theory. Nine states—Arizona, California, Idaho, Louisiana, Nevada, New Mexico, Texas, Washington, and Wisconsin— consider marital property community property. Under the common law theory, each spouse is an independent entity with ownership rights. Under the community property theory, all marital property is owned equally by both spouses, who have ownership over everything in the marital estate. While the laws in community property states have become a bit more liberal over time, there are still essential distinctions to discuss with your lawyer if you live in one of those community property states. Entire books have been written about the difference. Not very interesting books, I might add.

REAL PROPERTY

The law treats real estate differently than personal property—in part because of the permanency of real property and in part because of the old common law ideas surrounding ownership. Back in the days of early British common law, all land belonged to the king unless he granted some portion to you. Those land grants were so crucial to the king's subjects that they soon saw the necessity of documenting those transactions. After a while, they also began buying and selling those grants, which led to a central rule called the Statute of Frauds. That rule says that all real property transactions must be in writing. In many jurisdictions, the Statute of Frauds has been expanded to include any contract for goods valued more than $500 and for obligations lasting more than one year.

When you purchased your home, you went to the title company, or a notary came to you with all the documents. You then signed papers until you were tired, hungry, and had to pee. You signed volumes of documents because, over the years, land transactions have become complex affairs. The most important of all those documents is the deed and conveyance. The rest of the paper is to satisfy lenders and regulatory agencies. If you bought your home jointly with your spouse, both of you are listed on the deed that gives you ownership of the property. You also probably took out a joint mortgage to pay for the property. The terms of a mortgage are simple: you and your spouse agree to make the monthly payments and keep the property insured against loss. In return, the mortgage company lends you the money to purchase the house. The monthly payment you make to the mortgage company includes interest. That's their compensation for lending you the money.

The deed and the mortgage are two separate things, and that sometimes complicates property settlements. For instance, when Greg and Jennifer get married, Greg already owns a home, and Jennifer moves in. In a romantic gesture, Greg adds Jennifer to the deed of the property. She is now a legal owner of the property. Greg can't add Jennifer to the mortgage, though; that's something only the mortgage company can do. In general, adding or removing someone on a mortgage requires a complete refinance. Greg and Jennifer never get around to the refinance, and several years later, they divorce. Now, Jennifer is an owner but has no obligation to the lender to pay the mortgage. She also has the power to stop Greg from refinancing the property because the lender will require all legal owners' permission.

Real property is most often a couple's most significant asset, but houses are also homes. In addition to the monetary value of the property, there are emotional and practical considerations. You find yourself with most of your wealth tied up in a home that your children need. Now what? Balancing those choices might be difficult. It could require some creativity and demand patience and sacrifice from you. Again, don't shoot the messenger.

Here are some common ways that divorcing couples solve the problem:

- Establish the value of the home at the time of the divorce. Agree that one party will remain in the home for some time (one year, five years, until the youngest child graduates high school). The party who stays in the home will make all the mortgage payments and pay for the home's upkeep. At the end of the agreed period, they will sell the house. The spouse who is not living in the home will receive half the equity in the property at the time of the divorce, plus interest. The spouse who has been living in the home will receive the remainder, including any increase in the home's value. The reason is that the spouse living in the home has made all the payments, resulting in a reduction in the balance owing, and has also paid for improvements and upkeep.
- Establish the value of the home at the time of the divorce. Agree that one person will be awarded the home as their property. The person who is awarded the house must refinance the home within a reasonable time (often 90 or 120 days) to remove the other spouse from the mortgage and borrow enough money to pay them for their half of the equity.

PERSONAL PROPERTY

The personal property division can be just as complicated and emotional. The only thing people fight over more than their children is their stuff. Let's start with a ground rule for your stuff: Your stuff is not worth what you paid for it. Your stuff is worth what you could sell it for at a garage sale. I don't care if you spent a lot on your ten-year-old television, it's not worth what you paid for it ten years ago, and it's not worth what it would cost to replace it. The only exception could be collectible things. If you bought a Mickey Mantle rookie card to round out your extensive baseball card collection, it's undoubtedly worth more than when you bought it; the individual card not only has appreciated in value but also probably made your entire collection worth more. It's why we put collectibles and art in a different category. Reproductions and prints aren't collectible art unless you happen to have a limited edition Picasso print signed by the artist. In that case, you might want to have it appraised. And yes, I actually had a client who had one. Gifts are not marital property. If you surprised him with a Porsche on his birthday, it's his. You can't later take the gift back or demand your half.

Clients often have questions about the engagement ring, usually because the ring was an expensive purchase. The way we treat engagement rings is yet another relic of British common law that survived tossing the tea overboard. In traditional contract law, there must be someone who makes an offer, someone who accepts the offer, and something of value, called consideration, exchanged. In merry old England, an engagement was seen as a contract, and the ring was the consideration for the contract to marry. In general, a divorcing person's engagement ring is their property and doesn't go on the property list.

How do you begin to divide all the stuff? If you are still living in the home, go through the house and make a complete inventory. Group the things in your kitchen together by cupboard or drawer. The most difficult things to divide will be those with sentimental value. Most families struggle with how to divide Christmas decorations, photographs, and family heirlooms. If you are not still living in the home, try to visualize the things in the house and make a list. Don't forget to include the contents of your safe or bank safe deposit box.

Airline miles are also personal property, as are points in vacation rentals or timeshares. Individual airlines control when and how their air miles may be divided. Timeshares often result in the spouses playing a game of hot potato. "I don't want it; you keep it. No, I don't want it; you keep it." Timeshares often carry a lot of obligations with little value. The organization probably requires that you pay individual membership or homeowner dues and pay for your use of "your" unit. Timeshares are not a vacation home that you own; they are the right to rent a vacation home for some period. There are commercial companies that help you rid yourself of or even purchase timeshares. In either case, usually, the best you can hope for is to break even.

If there is a dispute over what an item is worth, the judge might order a property appraisal. These appraisals are only worth the expense if you own a lot of high-value assets. Many couples have their real property appraised, but some go further and have their personal property appraised. The appraisals may be helpful if you are dividing farm property, collectibles, or art.

I could fill this book with stories of disputes over personal property, but I'll illustrate with just a few. I recall the client who was ready to go to war over an antique stove. The stove symbolized all her hopes for the marriage and all the disappointments. My client and her husband had restored a lovely Victorian home, and my client had scoured the internet, thrift shops, and junk stores until she found the perfect period-appropriate antique iron stove for the kitchen. After spending many hours with wire brushes cleaning and refurbishing the stove, she had it painted bright red. The stove was the centerpiece of the restoration. To my client, the stove represented not only all the hard work that had gone into the restoration but also all the hard work that had gone into her marriage. Now that they were divorcing, they had decided to sell the home. The massive red stove was just another selling feature to the husband, but to my client, it was so much more. After much discussion about the cost and logistics of moving the massive stove versus the value of selling it with the house, my client agreed to leave the stove, but not before she asked for access to the house to have a professional photographer take its portrait.

Shortly before I retired from practice, I had a client who came to me for a divorce. She described her husband as controlling and mean.

Her husband wasn't physically abusive, but she said he manipulated and controlled her with money. The husband had a successful job. Since their children had left home, the wife started work at a part-time job. My client was a stylish woman who really liked nice clothes. When she left home, she wasn't able to take her extensive wardrobe with her. One of the first things she asked me was, "When can I get in the house to get the rest of my things?" We made arrangements for her to have access to the house to get her remaining things. She called me that afternoon, upset. It seems her husband had taken her most prized possession: a pair of Jimmy Choo shoes. Now, dear reader, this is not something I can relate to. I don't even remember when the moment happened, but a while back, I stopped standing in my closet asking, "What will make me look hot?" Instead, I started asking, "What will make me look presentable?" That's right; I'm that woman.

Nevertheless, I made a call to the husband's attorney and asked for the return of the Jimmy Choos. There ensued much wrangling over whether they were a gift to the wife or a purchase for "investment" purposes. The husband was adamant that he was only holding the shoes to ensure they were safe. Two weeks later, my client called me to announce that she and her husband were reconciling. She had agreed to return to the home and start marriage counseling in return for her husband giving her the Jimmy Choos back. This doesn't necessarily mean they stayed together, however; sometimes clients are too embarrassed to return to a lawyer when their reconciliation doesn't work.

All divorce lawyers' practices are littered with stories about property disputes because we give our possessions such meaning! Probably my most frustrating property case involved a blue crystal bowl. The spouses had been married for about five years, and there were significant problems in the marriage. They didn't have children, and they were able to agree quickly on nearly everything. They decided on what to do with their home and all the significant joint assets and debts. What they couldn't agree on was who would get a particular blue crystal bowl. The bowl was nothing special. You can find similar bowls online for under $100, but my client was adamant; he must have the bowl. He would never tell me why, just that it was a matter of principle. Whenever a client tells their lawyer, "it's a matter of principle," things are about to go expensively sideways. I tried to talk my client out of it. I even suggested he buy a replacement. Nothing worked, and because they couldn't reach an agreement about the bowl, my client decided to back out of the entire settlement, and we went to trial.

Judges and lawyers are busy—and most of us hate these sorts of trials—but the client has the right to demand one. I warned the client he ran the risk of making a judge angry over his pettiness. On the morning of the trial, we submitted our inventory lists and our proposed distributions. The clients took the witness stand, and the judge then laboriously went over every item with each spouse, which didn't do the judge's mood any good. In the end, it all came down to the blue crystal bowl. The wife took the stand and said she wanted the blue bowl; she liked it, and she used it all the time. My client then got on the stand and demanded the return of the blue crystal bowl. He told the judge the bowl had been a wedding gift from his sister, and since the marriage had not lasted, he believed he had a moral obligation to return the bowl to his sister. You can't make this stuff up. The judge awarded the wife the bowl, and, because the husband had been so stubborn, the judge ordered him to pay the wife's attorney fees. The blue crystal bowl cost my client a total of $20,000 in both his and his wife's attorney fees.

BUSINESSES AND OTHER TYPES OF PROPERTY

When most people think of property, they think of the tangible things in their home, but retirement accounts that are not in payout status, bank accounts, businesses, licenses, taxi medallions, fishing rights, air miles, farm subsidies, copyrights and patents, royalties, and stock options all fall into the category of property. In some states, professional degrees are also treated as property.

If you and your spouse own a business, how do you go about dividing it? The division of a business must be handled with utmost care. Involving an attorney who specializes in buying, selling, and dividing businesses may be wise because neither of you wants to destroy the source of your income in the process of your divorce. Unwinding the complications of a joint business can feel like a second divorce. There are many different kinds of businesses, and each has its own considerations. Say you and your spouse own a paint store. Determining the value of the business is pretty straightforward. The business's value is easily determined by looking at how much paint you've sold, how much inventory you have on hand, and how popular your store is with customers—the so-called "blue-sky" factor. If, on the other hand, your soon-to-be ex-spouse is a dentist, the valuation is trickier. The business's value isn't in how many root canals they've performed in the past year. The business value is determined by such things as the number of patients the office averages and something far less tangible: how hard the professional is willing to work. If you and your spouse own a joint business, it's probably best to hire an expert to tell you what the business is worth. It's also possible a judge could divide your family business interest and then order you to pay spousal support on top of it, meaning the receiving partner retains their interest in the business and receives a part of your business income stream.

Intellectual property is property, and if it was created during the marriage, it's marital property. Yes, you may be the one who developed the groundbreaking medical device or wrote the best seller. Still, your spouse is the one who fed the cat, took out the garbage, and mowed the lawn while you were busy creating, so the copyright or the patent is divisible property. If you received the patent or the copyright before the marriage, it remains your separate property, but any payments or royalties you received during the marriage are joint property.

The law favors finality. For that reason, property settlements aren't modifiable once they are final. The only exception is if there has been fraud or a failure to disclose an asset. Be sure and read chapter 15 if you're tempted to hide assets, especially if you're tempted to hide them in your business.

If you have a prenuptial agreement, the agreement could change the basic rules of property division, including those surrounding the division of your business. For information about prenuptial agreements, see chapter 15.

In states that still allow findings of fault in divorce, a judge can divide property in a way that punishes one spouse or the other. In those states, if the petitioner alleges and proves at trial that the other spouse has wronged them and therefore is at fault for the divorce, the judge can award more property to the wronged spouse.

17

RETIREMENT AND INVESTMENT ACCOUNTS, WILLS, AND TRUSTS

RETIREMENT AND INVESTMENT ACCOUNTS

Retirement and investment accounts are a form of property, but they rate their own chapter because they are so complex. There are many different retirement accounts, but they fall into two categories: defined benefit and defined contribution.

The **defined-benefit plan** is the kind of pension we usually think of, where a person works a certain number of years and receives a monthly income after retirement. Federal, state, military, railroad, Social Security, and union plans are all defined-benefit plans. Some plans require the beneficiary (the person receiving the payment) to contribute to their fund. Most require that you work a certain amount of time before the benefits are available to you. That's called "vesting." If you or your spouse are members of the U.S. military, you are entitled to retire with benefits after twenty years of service. Until you serve those twenty years, your benefit is not vested. If you leave the service at nineteen years and six months, you get nothing. Some federal and state benefits vest after ten or fifteen years of employment, and some plans partially vest in five-year increments. The benefit you receive when you retire depends on how many years you worked for the organization and the highest wage you earned in the last few years of that employment. Defined-benefit plans, particularly those offered to state employees, can be deceiving. The actual value of the fund could be far greater than the value on the annual statement. You must hire an expert to determine the actual value of a defined-benefit retirement fund. Actuaries compute the value of pensions and charge between $400 and $600 for each fund.

A **defined-contribution** plan is different. Plans like 401(k), 403(b), Thrift Savings Plans, and individual retirement accounts (IRAs) are examples of defined-contribution plans. Under these plans, money accumulates in an account and earns interest. You contribute a percentage of your income to the fund. The amount of your contribution is capped by federal rules, and your employer can match your contribution. You are eligible to draw out the funds when you reach age fifty-nine and a half. You may be able to withdraw money from that account earlier in a pinch, but there are steep penalties and taxes on the amount you withdraw. These fees and penalties are designed to discourage you from looting your future retirement to pay today's expenses. You could lose up to half of the account to the government in taxes, penalties, and fees. Many plans offer you the option to take a loan out, using your fund balance as collateral. Those loans can be a real lifesaver in an emergency but will be included in your divorce settlement as a debt. If you declare bankruptcy, the bankruptcy court can't force you to liquidate retirement funds to pay your debt.

Depending on your employer, you may have a 401(k) plan or a 403(b) plan; 401(k) plans are available for most companies, and 403(b) plans are available for nonprofit organizations such as hospitals, school districts, and charitable organizations. Many groups that offer defined-benefit plans, such as unions, also give employees the option of funding an additional Thrift Savings Plan. The plans operate like a 401(k).

Some employers offer stock options. Stock options are a tricky species of investment that requires special consideration. Stock options are the opportunity in the future to buy your employer's stock at the value at the time of the award. Options can be valuable if the stock price has increased or the stock has split. An employer might offer options for several reasons. They are offered as a signing bonus when an employee starts with the company. They can also award employees for good performance, but most commonly, employers give out stock options as an incentive to stay with the company. This kind of stock option is often called "golden handcuffs." The formula for dividing any stock options is called the time rule. Don't let the math freak you out.

Here is the most common formula, and it's used when the stock options were awarded to encourage an employee to remain with the company. The formula looks like this:

$$\frac{\text{DOA} - \text{DOS}}{\text{DOA} - \text{DOV}} \times \text{Number of shares exercisable} = \text{Community Property Shares}$$

(DOA = Date of Award; DOS = Date of Separation; DOV = Date of Vesting)

I feel the panic in your eyes, so at the risk of causing a full-blown story-problem-induced psychosis, let's put this into context. Let's say Jenny is offered a job at a tech company, and as an incentive, they offer her an option to buy 100 shares of stock in four years. The offer allows her to pay the value when she started, which should, if Jenny's been doing her job, be substantially lower than the current price of the stock. Jenny receives the stock options on January 1, 2020. The options are to vest on January 1, 2024, but she and Lenny separate two years later, on January 1, 2022. Using a handy online calculator, we know that there have been 731 days from the date of the stock option grant until she and Lenny separated and that there are 1,461 days between the date the options were granted and the date the option will vest. The formula looks like this: $731 \div 1,461 \times 100 = 50.34$, which means 50.34 shares are marital property.

There are many other formulas, depending on the reason for the award of the options and the state in which you live. Your attorney will advise you as to which formula applies to your specific situation. It's enough that you know that stock options are marital property and that the proper formula must be used in your particular situation to determine the number of shares each of you is entitled to.

Many people also have private investment accounts. Those accounts could be in the form of stocks and bonds managed through a brokerage, Certificates of Deposit (CD), or mutual funds. As a rule, any portion of a fund accumulated during the marriage is marital property, as is any increase in value during the marriage. If, for example, you had a mutual fund that contained $1,000 when you married and now contains $10,000 at the time of your divorce, the original $1,000 balance is your separate property. Any increase in the value from either contributions or interest is marital property. In this case, $9,000 of the fund is divisible. So you would receive $4,500 + $1,000 = $5,500, while your spouse would receive $4,500. The same rule applies to retirement accounts—any contributions you made to a retirement fund before your marriage remains your separate property. Any contributions and any increase in value that occurred during the marriage will be divided equally. When you are dealing with retirement accounts, it's best to have an expert, called an actuary, determine the actual value of the fund, which portions are divisible, and the exact dollar amounts of each share. Actuaries charge between $200 and $400 per account to perform those calculations.

As we discovered earlier, retirement funds are subject to federal rules, including the federal tax code. Withdrawing money can have financial consequences. A retirement account division due to divorce is not a withdrawal as long as you do it right. The federal rules require a separate court order called a Qualified Domestic Relations Order (QDRO) to be signed by a judge before retirement accounts are divided without penalty. People often equalize the award of retirement funds by offsetting them with other assets to avoid paying for a QDRO. For example, one spouse may take the entire pension and less equity from the family home in exchange.

I realize that a few wonks will find this fascinating, but most people's eyes have glazed over at this point. You don't have to understand how the time rule works or the intricacies of a QDRO, but you do need to know enough to ask your lawyer about them.

Retirement and Spousal Support

Retirement is often a consideration when determining spousal support. Lawyers consider the relative position of the parties once they retire. Often, there is a substantial inequality in post-retirement income that must be equalized. It would be unfair for a spouse who remained home and cared for the children to be disadvantaged at retirement in long-term marriages; that can mean a spousal support obligation that continues after retirement, although it may be at a reduced rate.

WILLS AND TRUSTS

Wills and other estate planning are the most ignored and overlooked details in life. By some estimates, nearly half of all Americans do not have a will. Believe me, the people you leave behind won't thank you for not getting around to making a will. It's not a fun thing to think about, but since we are doing many hard things here, do it anyway.

Wills are one of the most formal and ceremonial things that law dictates. State laws differ on whether you can leave a handwritten will. Check your jurisdiction before you decide to handwrite your will. Even if you and your spouse have wills, divorce changes everything. When possible, you should complete a new will as soon as possible after your divorce judgment is filed. Also, do everyone a favor and shred the old one so there is no dispute about which one is valid.

The most important consideration is who will take care of your minor children if you die. In most states, the other parent becomes the custodial parent if you die. Because of the constitutional preference for biological parents (see the discussion of *Troxel v. Granville* in chapter 9), it's not possible to make a legally binding award of custody in your will. You can and should express your preference in your will if you believe someone other than your child's other parent should have custody.

Many states require that the parent paying child support have life insurance to replace their support should they die while they still have a child support obligation. Ideally, both parents should have life insurance to ensure their children are cared for if they die before the children are adults. If you have life insurance, you should change the beneficiary to your child, IN TRUST. That means that a trustee will be appointed to manage your child's money. That's important because a trustee, even if it's your child's other parent, has a fiduciary duty to act in the child's best interest when managing their money. If you don't believe your former spouse will manage your child's money appropriately, name someone else as trustee. You may also want to appoint an independent trustee if you are concerned about your former spouse having custody of your child after your death. If you remove the financial incentive for your ex to pursue custody, it often reduces the chance they will put up a fight if the child is placed with another relative instead.

Do your children—and the person who will be taking care of things if you die—a big favor. Execute a new will as soon as your divorce is final, which includes a trust (often called a pour-over trust) for your children. The proceeds of your estate fund the pour-over trust. Ensure that you change the beneficiary on all your bank accounts and retirement accounts, including your IRAs and any Certificates of Deposit (CDs).

If you and/or your spouse succumbed to the living trust craze of the past decade, be sure that you dissolve your living trust and move all your assets back into your name. Living trusts were sold as a way to avoid probate when you die. Realistically, they were only helpful in large estates, but lawyers and insurance brokers made bundles off of convincing people they needed them. A living trust requires that you transfer all your property into the trust. If you have one, you need to ensure that the titles of all your property and accounts are transferred back to you and your spouse's individual names and that the trust is dissolved. Be sure to let your lawyer know you have a living trust and give them a copy of the trust documents.

18

MEDIATION

Before you rush to the courthouse and a trial, your lawyer may suggest mediation, or your court may require it. What's mediation? It's when you and your spouse sit down with a third party and try to reach an agreement. You may be thinking, "If I could sit down and discuss things with my spouse, we wouldn't be getting divorced." And you probably would be right if it were just the two of you; however, mediation is a specialized kind of meeting with your spouse, and the third party isn't a friend or your brother-in-law. A mediator is a person who has received training to manage these sorts of meetings.

Mediation is not marriage counseling, and it's not a meeting to air your grievances or discuss your relationship. It's a meeting to do the hard work of wrapping up the business end of your divorce, and it's a good step to try before resorting to a trial.

No one knows more about you and your spouse and is better qualified to make decisions for your family than you two. A good mediator can help you navigate the volatile parts of the relationship until you reach an agreement. There are a few different ways mediation can help, and there are several different types of mediators. Judges often order parents to at least try to mediate custody and parenting-time disputes, and some states and counties require it. Mediators can be lawyers or therapists. It's important to understand the difference and when one might be better than the other.

You can mediate your entire divorce, including decisions about property, debt, and support. If you intend to mediate all those issues, it's essential your mediator also be a lawyer. The mediator you hire can't also be your lawyer because the mediator must be a disinterested third party who doesn't owe loyalty to either of you. Many lawyers train to do family law mediation. If you are using a lawyer mediator to help resolve your entire divorce, expect to provide the mediator with the same information you would be expected to present to the court, including all your financial records. Mediators don't make decisions for you. They help you and your spouse look at all the facts, think about the circumstances, consider what a judge might do at trial, and make a decision for yourselves. Agreements made in mediation are not binding until they are reduced to writing and signed by both parties. Your mediation negotiation is confidential and not admissible in court if you later have a trial.

Couples choose mediation because it is less expensive than a trial. In many jurisdictions, the court or a city or county agency offers mediation on a sliding-fee scale. Even if you choose a lawyer mediator who charges $300 per hour, your cost to resolve the case will be substantially less than if you have a trial.

Divorcing couples often experience an imbalance in the emotional power in the relationship. The imbalance might be the reason for the divorce, or it can arise when one spouse wants the divorce and the other doesn't. Negotiation is impossible unless both parties have some power and agency, so your mediator's training helps them balance the emotional power in the room so that each partner can be heard and have their needs met. It's imperative you let your mediator know if you have experienced domestic violence in your relationship. Mediation is still possible but will be done using different strategies and techniques. For example, the mediator might decide to have each of you in a separate room and shuttle back and forth between you rather than have you present together. Many mediators can conduct sessions via video conference; it's helpful in volatile cases since the mediator can control who is on the call at any one time.

Not every mediation is successful. You may both try your best in mediation and still not be able to reach an agreement. If that happens, your lawyer will notify the court that mediation was not successful and ask the court to set a trial date.

Couples often include a provision in their final divorce judgment that requires them to try mediation before they go back to court to modify the terms of custody, parenting time, and support. The requirement can be helpful or may just put up a roadblock to getting into court. Couples who found mediation useful the first time will likely turn to mediation to resolve a later problem. If mediation was not helpful, or if one party tried to use it to manipulate the other, you may consider asking that the requirement to mediate is omitted.

19

TRIALS AND TRIBULATIONS

WILL IT EVER END?

The moment will come when you stand in your wailing wall shower and wonder if your divorce will ever end. You weren't at all prepared for the financial and emotional toll it's taken as it drags on. There will have been so many delays and false starts that you think you might scream, lose your mind, or both.

Court scheduling is frustrating and sometimes inexplicable. Some even speculate that all court scheduling is done in a basement by three grizzled women stirring a large cauldron while using tarot cards and a handful of chicken bones. Others say it's one big Excel spreadsheet designed to inflict the most misery and inconvenience possible. Either might be right.

Every court has its own scheduling rubric, which controls which cases get priority. Courts typically schedule cases in this order:

- Criminal cases where the defendant is in custody and constitutionally entitled to a speedy trial, including juvenile cases.
- Challenges to family abuse restraining orders (in most states, there are strict rules on how soon they must hold a hearing).
- Child welfare shelter hearings for the initial removal of children into foster care.
- Child welfare hearings to challenge the initial removal of children into foster care.
- Mental health commitment hearings.
- Family law cases involving custody of children and criminal cases where the defendant is out of custody.

- Civil cases including auto accidents, medical malpractice, business and contract disputes, and divorces without children.

Within each category, the court will schedule trials starting with the oldest case. In between all the trials, judges also hear motions and other short matters. They hear things like probation violation hearings, discovery motions, restraining order petitions, small claims cases, violations of restraining orders, and criminal motions such as motions to suppress evidence and challenges to searches and seizures. They also meet with law enforcement to review and approve search warrants. Judges share the responsibility of being on call after hours to review search warrants. In other words, there's plenty of work to go around.

There is no question most courts are overloaded. The funding of new judicial positions and for new or expanded courthouses usually lags behind the need by several years, if not decades. Scheduling problems frustratingly compound when cases settle the day before, or even on the morning of trial, leaving an overscheduled courtroom suddenly empty. Court staff uses their best information to forecast and schedule, but the system is still imperfect. What that means for you is that it's not unusual to have a scheduled court date "bumped" by the court, sometimes more than once, in favor of higher priority cases. It's especially frustrating and expensive when either you or your witnesses must travel to appear at the trial or if you have scheduled experts to testify.

Your attorney does a lot of work to prepare for your trial. They research the applicable law, apply it to your case's facts, and then assemble documents and witnesses to support their theory of your case. If you've chosen your lawyer well, it's exacting, detailed work. Your lawyer compiles all this information, including all your most current bank statements, bills, and other documents. If your trial gets bumped by several weeks, your lawyer must move on to prepare for other trials. That means when your trial comes up again, your lawyer must do some of the preparation over again. Your lawyer has to update all the documents to be sure they have the most current information. They will need to make sure the cases they're basing their argument on haven't been overruled, and they need to refamiliarize themselves with the facts of your case. While a good lawyer may make you feel like your case is their only one, in reality, your attorney has other clients. In my years of practice, I averaged a mix of one hundred open juvenile, criminal, and family law cases at any given time. When your attorney knows there's a less than 50 percent chance your scheduled trial will actually be heard, it can be like a game of high-stakes chicken. How much of your client's money do you spend preparing for a trial that probably will not happen? But what if, by some miracle, it does happen?

When you need a trial because you've tried but couldn't settle your case, how do you avoid this frustration and get your case in front of a judge? You rent one. That's right, in most states, you can hire a private judge. You can't just hire anyone to be your judge; your private judge must be certified by the state and is usually a judge who has retired from the active bench. They only hear cases that don't require juries. A private judge isn't cheap but has its advantages: your trial date is certain, and your trial can remain confidential. Courthouse proceedings, except for some juvenile cases, are open to the public, so if you want to keep the details of your divorce on the down low, hiring a judge is your best choice. Your trial will be held in a lawyer's conference room rather than in a courtroom. The same rules of evidence and the same courtroom protocols apply if you hire a private judge and you have all of the same rights on appeal. Hiring a judge is not the same as buying justice. If you hire a retired judge, you should split the cost with your ex if possible. You should expect the judge to render a fair and proper judgment according to the law, regardless of who pays the bill. And yes, it is an option open only to the privileged.

PREPARING FOR TRIAL

In any given year, between 90 and 95 percent of divorces settle before trial. Despite your best efforts at mediation or negotiation, you haven't been able to resolve the disputes in your divorce, and you find yourself in the 5 percent with a trial date approaching. What happens next? Don't skip this chapter because you are at the beginning of divorce; this chapter is an essential guidepost for what to expect and how to avoid trial.

Only Georgia and Texas permit jury trials in divorce cases. Only Texas allows a jury to determine which parent will have custody. Texas also allows a jury to decide which property is marital and which is not.

In all other states, a judge will decide your divorce. When you choose to have a trial, you are paying a lawyer to educate themselves about your specific situation and how the law applies to it so they can educate a judge about all the details in a few hours at trial. Your lawyer will not cover every subtle detail, and the judge will not understand everything perfectly. Instead, your lawyer will present the essential information and ask the judge to decide who will have custody of your children, who will receive what property, who will pay which debts, and whether one of you will pay child or spousal support.

Preparing for trial is a significant and costly undertaking. You can count on being in court seven hours per trial day, and your lawyer could need as much as three or four hours of preparation for each hour in court. You should expect each day of trial to cost an average of ten hours of advanced preparation. You might also need to hire experts to provide the judge with information on specific issues, such as who should receive custody or what a business or a home is worth.

TRIAL EXPERTS

Let's look at some of the types of experts you might need at trial.

Custody

If you and your spouse can't agree on child custody, it will be up to a judge to decide what is in your children's best interest. Judges decide a dispute based on the best information they have at hand, and they welcome the opinions of experts. If you are disputing custody, you may want to complete a custody and parenting-time evaluation. The evaluation is a comprehensive study done by a professional. Most evaluators are doctors of psychology, although some may come from other mental health disciplines. Individual state law may determine who can perform custody evaluations. A good forensic assessment will include psychological and personality testing of each parent and any stepparents or new partners, interviews with the parents and any new partners, interviews with the children, observed sessions either in the office or in the home evaluating the interaction between each parent and the children, review of any relevant medical and mental health records for the parents or the children, and conversations with collateral sources including personal references, the children's teachers, and the parents' and children's doctors or therapists. Once the evaluator gathers all the information, they write a comprehensive report, recommending which parent should have legal custody and suggesting a parenting schedule. On average, custody evaluations cost between $3,000 and $10,000, depending on the case's complexity. Usually, that fee will not include travel or the cost of your evaluator coming to court to testify. If your lawyer calls the evaluator as a witness, they will likely charge you by the hour for their time to appear in court, plus any travel expenses. You might ask, "Why spend the money?" Because custody evaluations often push an otherwise unresolvable case to settlement. Judges place great weight on experts' opinions, and it's unusual for a judge to disregard an expert recommendation. Once you have an evaluation, it can move the case to settlement by resolving the critical issue of custody.

Property

There are a few different types of experts you might need to inform the court about your property.

REAL PROPERTY

If there is a dispute about your real estate's value, you will need a property appraisal, which is an evaluation done by a person who is licensed to inspect and evaluate your home and determine what it's worth. The expert will look at your home and compare it with others in your neighborhood, including homes that have recently sold. A property appraisal should cost between $400 and $800, depending upon your location and the evaluation's complexity. Your appraiser will probably charge an additional fee for appearing in court to testify. Sometimes you can get by with a realtor who does a market analysis, as long as both you and your spouse agree to use the value the realtor gives you.

PERSONAL PROPERTY

The kind of expert you need depends on the property you are evaluating. There are experts who specialize in appraising art, firearms and weapons, automobiles, antiques, collectibles, jewelry, and farm equipment and livestock. Each of them charges differently depending on their time and expertise. As I cautioned earlier, judges will value property at garage-sale value unless there is a reason not to. Your grandfather's baseball card collection may be worth a lot, but your Beanie Babies collection probably is not, no matter how many little plastic heart-shaped tag covers you used. If you believe you have valuable things, you should begin by doing a bit of research online. Start with sites like eBay, where the free market sets the price. That will give you a rough idea of the value. If the property's value justifies the expense, have them professionally appraised.

BUSINESSES

If you or your spouse owns a business, some or all it may be considered marital property. Any portion of the business created during the marriage is marital property. But businesses are not static things like houses or cars. Business success waxes and wanes with the overall success of the economy, and to further complicate things, there are many different kinds of businesses. A lawyer or a dentist in a solo practice is vastly different from a retail business. With a professional practice, the business value is based upon the principal's experience, training, reputation, and how hard they are willing to work. The judge may have to sort out whether the business is property or just income potential.

In contrast, a retail business's value is based primarily on how much inventory is on hand, the profit margin on the sold goods, and past sales history. Having a business valuation done by a qualified business evaluator will help the judge make a fair decision. It's especially imperative if the business is the primary source of income in your marriage.

Income and Income Potential

Spouses often disagree about how much the other spouse makes or how much they could make. In that case, it's sometimes necessary to bring in an expert. I've had many cases where one spouse left the workforce to be the primary caregiver for the couple's children; yet, on divorce, the employed spouse either thinks the homemaker should return to work immediately at the same level they left or otherwise overestimates the homemaker's income potential. In that case, you should hire an expert to evaluate the spouse's earning potential and testify to it in court. Income and earning specialists can also be necessary if one spouse is underemployed. I saw a case where a neurosurgeon took a job in medical sales to lower his income before his divorce and a case where a woman with a PhD in education claimed she only obtained her education to homeschool her children. The teacher claimed she needed support to remain at home and homeschool the parties' children. The neurosurgeon claimed the judge should set the wife's spousal support based on his sales job's much lower income. The judge, in that case, found the neurosurgeon could make more in his chosen profession than in sales and set his support based on his income as a neurosurgeon. A judge also found that the teacher could work in her profession, although probably not at the level that the husband thought. The judge found she could and should work as a classroom teacher and set support based on the assumption that she could make an annual salary equal to that of a starting teacher in her district. The judge also found that there was no compelling reason to continue homeschooling the children. As an aside, judges generally don't object to homeschooling but won't order that one parent support the other financially to continue homeschooling unless there is some reason the child can't attend public school.

Most states have rules governing bad faith. Remember that bundle of marital rights we talked about at the beginning? Well, there are responsibilities in the bundle, too. One of those is called a fiduciary duty. A fiduciary duty is a legal and ethical responsibility to be loyal and act in the other person's best interest. It's an obligation of honesty and fair dealing. Your banker and your lawyer have a fiduciary duty to you, and you and your spouse have a fiduciary duty to each other. That fiduciary duty doesn't end until the final divorce judgment is signed, and if you violate your duty to your spouse, a judge can find you acted in bad faith.

In many states, a judge can impose consequences for bad faith, such as awarding your spouse more of the assets as compensation. Remember **Rule 6**: ***Don't hide income, property, or debt.***

Income Taxes

There are times when you may need to call in an expert on income taxes, although it's less common these days. Until recently, lawyers called tax experts as witnesses to present evidence on the tax consequences of spousal support. In the past, spousal support was considered income to the receiving spouse, and the paying spouse got a write-off. Recent revisions in the tax code have done away with that rule. Both child and spousal support now pass between spouses without any tax consequence. Tax rules change frequently, and I always advise my clients to meet with a tax advisor to create a post-divorce tax plan. In general, the property division in a divorce is not a taxable event, but there are exceptions. There may be taxes to pay on those transactions if you sell the marital home or cash out stock options or retirement funds. The testimony of a tax expert can assist the judge in allocating tax liability in those cases.

OTHER TRIAL WITNESSES

Do you think you need character witnesses? With the rise of no-fault divorce rules, lawyers use character witnesses less and less. If child custody is an issue, one or two witnesses who can testify to your involvement with your children and your skills as a parent may help the judge. Those witnesses should not be your parents or siblings because most judges assume your family will support you. The exception would be if a family member saw or heard a domestic violence incident or was the person you confided in after such an incident.

It's sometimes necessary to call witnesses to testify to your spouse's lack of parenting interest or ability. In general, judges don't like pissing contests and dueling character witnesses. If you must call a character witness, be sure that the person is credible, that they don't abuse drugs or alcohol, and that there are no recent arrests or scandals in their past. Even then, presenting witnesses solely to discredit your spouse can backfire. Say your client tells you she has a witness who can testify to her husband's lazy parenting. You chat with the witness, a nice older woman, who seems to have some persuasive information about how the father spends most of his day playing video games while the child sits in a playpen all day in a filthy diaper. On the witness stand, the witness tells the judge about the father's video game addiction. So far, so good. But then, God help you, she gets on a roll. She tells everyone how the child's father is having an incestuous affair with his mother and how she doesn't think the father's sister is a good influence either, because of all the time she spends helping the human traffickers who are tunneling in the basement. The moral: be absolutely sure you know what your witness is going to say.

Children as Witnesses

My short answer is *don't*. Remember **Rule 1**: *Whatever this shit is, it belongs to you. Don't make your shit your children's shit. Ever.* There is only one specific situation where I consider calling a child as a witness; that's when the child is the only witness of serious domestic violence. Note I used the word *serious*. Do not ever let your anger at your spouse or your desire to win cloud your judgment on this subject. Do not ask your child to tell the judge who they want to live with, even if your child insists they want to. Your child is not emotionally mature enough to handle the pressure, and you should not be asking them to. If you believe someone must communicate the children's position to the judge, consider having the child talk to a trusted therapist and have the therapist testify about the child's wishes.

Lawyers are required to follow their client's direction on how to try their case, even if they disagree. I have, at times, brought children into court as witnesses because my client insisted. I have also, at times, cautioned clients if they insisted on calling their children, I probably wasn't the right lawyer for them. I believe, in a handful of my cases, the children's testimony was essential to protect their safety as well as the safety of their parent. In those cases, the need outweighed the trauma to the child. In all the other instances where children testified, the need never proved to outweigh the damage to the children or the disdain the judge felt for my client.

TRIAL DAY

Here is what to expect on the day of your trial: You will be nervous. Your lawyer will probably suggest you arrive early. Get the best sleep you can the night before. Beware of taking something to help you sleep or having a few drinks to relax because you don't want to show up groggy or hungover.

Dress like you are going to church. It might seem obvious, but believe me when I say someone is reading this who will need these specifics: no skirts shorter than the top of the knee, no leggings or other skin-tight pants, no shirts that show cleavage, no hats, and no pants that sag and show your underwear; no tank tops, undershirts, bare midriffs, or T-shirts with print or with pictures or logos on them; no platform heels; and no fleece pajama bottoms, especially ones with the logo of your favorite heavy metal band or sports team. Over the years, I've had clients show up for court in some pretty interesting T-shirts. Take, for example, "I may be fat, but you're ugly, and I can diet," "Resist Authority," "You're stupid, but I'm cute," and of course, the "Don't Tread on Me" design popular with conservative activists. Those were the times I insisted my client attend their trial with their T-shirt on inside out and backward.

Take a shower that morning, shave, brush your teeth, and wear deodorant because you will be stress-sweating all day. Don't drink more than a couple of cups of coffee because, from the judge's bench, coffee jitters and meth jitters look a lot alike.

Your lawyer will probably suggest you arrive early on the morning of your trial. If you have never been to a courthouse before, your lawyer may also suggest you visit the courthouse in advance of your trial to familiarize yourself with your surroundings. Remember, your lawyer does this all the time, but you don't. Your lawyer will arrive with many files, probably a laptop, and perhaps some law books. Be sure you have a pad of paper and a pen to take notes and write questions to your lawyer. Your lawyer will have organized the necessary documents they will be presenting to the judge during the trial; these are called exhibits. They will have copies for the judge, the opposing attorney, and you. They will also make sure there is a copy on the witness stand for witnesses to use while they are testifying. Your lawyer will give the court clerk the original exhibits, who will keep track of them as the trial progresses. We'll talk more about exhibits as we discuss the rules of evidence. Most states call the parties in a divorce the Petitioner and the Respondent. The Petitioner is the person who filed the divorce petition, and the Respondent is the person who is responding to the petition. The Petitioner puts their case on first. Each lawyer will have the chance to make an opening statement. The Petitioner's lawyer will call witnesses and ask them questions in what is called direct examination. The Respondent then cross-examines the Petitioner's witness. The judge will then allow the Petitioner to ask rebuttal questions, and the Respondent can ask surrebuttal questions. The Respondent can only cross-examine a witness on subjects that the Petitioner covered in direct examination. Once the Petitioner has presented all their witnesses and evidence, the Respondent will begin their side of the case. They will call witnesses and ask direct questions, and the Petitioner will be able to cross-examine the witnesses. When both finish, each will make a closing argument. Each lawyer will lay out the facts and the law they think support the judge finding in their client's favor.

A trial is like a choreographed dance. Don't panic if you don't understand the steps; if you did your chapter 5 homework and hired a good lawyer, they know the steps. One of the most perplexing parts of the law for the nonlawyer is the rules of evidence. Rest assured, it's sometimes perplexing for lawyers, too. The rules about when and how evidence can be introduced at trial are complex and nuanced. Law students spend an entire year learning about the admissibility of evidence.

Your attorney can present evidence in many forms. Evidence can be witness testimony or a tangible thing like a document, photo, or recording. Most often, the facts in a case are presented by a combination of testimony and documents. Your lawyer might call a witness to talk about your earning capacity or introduce credit card statements to prove the amount of marital debt; photographs might be offered to illustrate your attachment to your children.

Evidence must be "admitted" to the trial record before the judge can consider it. There are specific rules about what evidence can be admitted for the judge to consider. The rules of evidence assure that the judge only considers the most reliable and truthful evidence during your trial. Your attorney will offer documentary evidence as exhibits.

Exhibits are numbered, and the clerk keeps a running record of them. The Petitioner uses numbers 1–99, and the Respondent uses 101–199. Your attorney will "offer" each exhibit. The judge will ask if there are any objections to the exhibit. The other attorney can either not object or explain why they believe the judge should not admit the evidence. The judge will then decide if the evidence can be considered, and if it can, the judge will say it's "received."

There are several basic concepts to understand about the admissibility of evidence:

Relevance. The information you present must be relevant to the question at hand. If you ask the judge to decide who should have custody of your child, the fact your child has a learning disability and you are the parent who regularly communicates with his teacher and his therapist is relevant. The fact your father served in the U.S. Navy is not. Only relevant evidence will be admitted and considered.

Hearsay. There's nothing more daunting for legal professionals than the rules surrounding hearsay. These complex rules were designed to assure that if something is asserted as truth, it's reliable. For instance, if you ask the judge to award you custody because your spouse's alcoholism is out of control, you can't testify a friend told you her husband said his friend said he saw your spouse drinking at the bar. The person who has the information has to come to court and testify. If a statement starts, "he told me," it's hearsay and will not be admitted. Likewise, you can't have your friend write you a letter telling the judge you're a good parent.

There are exceptions to the hearsay rule. Those exceptions are for information that either isn't offered for the hearsay's truth or has some "indicia of reliability." For example, consider a case about an injury that happened after people in a nightclub rushed the doors because they thought the place was on fire. The witness testifies, "I heard someone yell, 'fire'!" The statement isn't being offered to prove the club was on fire; it's offered to show the effect the statement had on the person who heard it. The other exception is for evidence whose reliability speaks for itself. An example would be a regularly kept business record, like a telephone bill or a police report.

The rules of evidence are the complicated tango at the heart of any trial; you will be confused by them. When the trial is underway, your lawyer is concentrating on making sure they present the big picture while following the individual steps of objections and the answers. If you have questions, it's best to jot them down, so your lawyer isn't distracted and can answer them as they are able.

Once the judge has heard all the evidence from both sides, they will make a decision. The judge may issue a ruling that day after a review of their notes. They may also take the case "under advisement," which means the judge will take some time to review the facts and the applicable law and then either issue a written opinion or schedule a time for you to come back to court to receive their oral decision.

The outcome of your trial is uncertain. Your lawyer can tell you what they expect. They can tell you their best guess based on their experience in similar cases and with the particular judge in your case. They don't have a crystal ball and can't tell you for sure what will happen. That's why your lawyer will encourage you to resolve the case without trial even if you have to compromise because when you do, you have some control over the outcome. In my experience, no one leaves a courtroom fully satisfied or wholly vindicated. Remember: the judge can't manufacture money or make your spouse a better parent or a nicer person.

Once the judge decides the case, they will also decide how the attorney fees for both of you will be paid. In general, each party pays their own fees. Still, the law in most states allows the judge to order one spouse to pay the other's legal fees if there is a significant difference in the incomes of the parties and the lower-earning spouse can demonstrate a financial need, or when one party has been unreasonable in their position. Take note of that last factor. If you take an unreasonable position not supported by the facts or the law, you will likely end up paying your spouse's attorney fees. Remember the story about the trial over a blue crystal bowl from chapter 16? In that case, my client insisted on a trial when he and his wife could not agree on who would keep a blue crystal bowl. My client lost the fight for the bowl and had to pay his wife's attorney fees for being unreasonable. In total, he spent about $20,000 to argue over a $60 blue bowl he didn't even win.

Once your trial judge issues a decision, it's final. You can't renegotiate, and you can't ask the judge to modify their findings. In most states, property divisions are final and can't be modified unless you can prove some kind of fraud. Child custody and parenting time, child support, and spousal support are modifiable if there has been a substantial change in circumstances since the court's last order. See chapter 20 for a complete discussion of modifications to your final divorce judgment. Some states still have a waiting period after divorce, during which you can't remarry. There is a difference between being unhappy with a judge's ruling and believing the judge made a mistake. When a judge makes an error, you have the option of filing an appeal. In most states, there are three levels of court. First, there is the trial court, where a case is initially decided. Then, there is the appeals court, where a panel of judges can review the trial court's decision. If you still believe the decision is wrong after the appeals court decides, you can appeal to the state supreme court. Not every court order is appealable; which decisions are appealable, and the way the appeals court reviews them, are narrow and specific. If you feel the judge's decision is in error, discuss it with your lawyer, who will know whether the facts of your case warrant an appeal.

Not all trial lawyers also work on appeals, so you will probably have to hire an appellate attorney if you appeal. Appeals are costly, and usually everyone pays their own attorney fees and costs. You must submit a written transcript of your trial to the appeals court, and it has to be completed by a certified transcriptionist. In divorce appeals, the expense is the responsibility of the person filing the appeal. Transcriptionists charge an average of $2.50 per page, and having a professional transcribe a lengthy trial can cost several thousand dollars. Once the transcription is finished, your attorney will then write an appellate brief. These briefs are long and detailed. They outline your argument as to why the trial judge's decision was wrong or was not based in law. Once your brief is filed, the other side will have the opportunity to file a brief in reply. If you thought your trial was slow, try waiting for an appeal. Your appeal may take one to three years to be decided. Sometimes appellate courts issue a stay, which keeps the trial court's underlying order from going into effect before they decide the dispute. That's especially important if the trial court's decision involves a change in your child's custody; you don't want the child bounced back and forth until there is a final decision.

After you reach an agreement or the judge issues a decision in your divorce trial, one of the attorneys will write the final divorce judgment. In some jurisdictions, an individual judge can adopt their own preferred language they require to be in any judgment they sign. In other jurisdictions, there may be uniform language the entire county or state has adopted. Your judgment is one of the most important documents in your life to this point, so it's critical to get it right. If you don't understand parts of your final judgment, don't approve it until your lawyer answers all your questions. I have included a sample of a divorce judgment in the document samples in appendix B at the end of the book. While it includes many of the most common provisions, it's not comprehensive. Not every judgment will contain every part of the sample, and your lawyer may suggest other provisions unique to your case. Your lawyer will also ensure the judgment contains any provisions required by your state law. Your parenting plan should either be included in your divorce judgment or attached as an exhibit.

It's critical to make sure the money judgment section of your divorce judgment is included and accurate. It's the portion of the document that gives you the authority to collect your child and spousal support and any other judgments for equalizing your property division.

Your trial will be difficult and emotional; as the trial date approaches, you may want to seek a counselor's support to work through your anxiety. Once your trial concludes, you will feel like you ran a marathon. Even if you win everything you asked for, your body, heart, and soul will feel weary and bruised. Grant yourself some grace, and don't beat yourself up if you overeat, drink a little too much wine, or sleep for a day. As always, this advice only applies if you are not in recovery from addiction. If you are, get to a meeting right away. Set aside time for counseling, time with friends and family, and, if needed, a debrief with your lawyer.

Whatever the judge decides at your trial, you've reached the finish line. Congratulations, you made it.

20

CH-CH-CHANGES, MODIFICATIONS, AND CONTEMPT

We humans have the bad habit of thinking things will never change. Think about it. How much has your life changed in the past five years? And yet, five years ago, you thought your life would always be the way it was then. The one certainty in life is change, and there is no bigger game changer than divorce. After a divorce, people start new careers, return to school, start new relationships, and in general, ch-ch-change (thank-you, David Bowie). Those changes often make your custody, support, and parenting-time plans outdated and irrelevant. That's when it's time for a modification.

Before you file a motion with the court to modify your divorce judgment, be sure to look over your original judgment. Some jurisdictions require that you mediate before you return to court. If your judgment requires you to mediate before you file an action with the court to modify it, be sure to schedule your mediation first. Prepare for mediation by collecting the same discovery information you will need for a trial, including financial records. In many cases, once you contact the mediator, they will contact your ex and invite them to a session. The mediator will outline the issues that need to be discussed and let your former spouse know what documents they will need to bring with them. You are not required to continue mediation if you don't reach an agreement in the first session, but you may agree to continue if you think you can get to an agreement with future sessions.

CHILD CUSTODY AND PARENTING TIME

Child custody is the area where most modifications start. Modifying child custody is not easy. Judges are hesitant to change a child's custody unless it is absolutely necessary. Judges will not change custody because you remarried, got a better job, moved into a nicer house, or can provide a better lifestyle for your children. The decision to change custody requires you to prove two things: first, you must prove there has been a substantial change in the circumstances that directly affect your child. It's the threshold question in nearly every jurisdiction. If you can't prove there has been some change in circumstances, then you don't even get to the second question of whether a change in custody is in your child's best interest. That second question, the best interest test, asks what is best for your child's physical and emotional health. You will have to prove it's best for your child that their life is radically upended. If your former spouse has joined a cult or become a meth-snorting biker chick, proving it may be pretty straightforward. But without a clear-cut reason, changing custody is an uphill battle.

One of the most common reasons people ask for a change in custody is that the custodial parent plans to or has moved away from the other parent. As I've said, changes in lifestyle and employment are common after divorce. The law about moving away is an area that is developing. It used to be the custodial parent called the shots, and the noncustodial parent had to accommodate those choices. Now, the law is a bit more nuanced. Some states, like Michigan, even restrict parents with joint or shared legal custody from moving more than one hundred miles from the other parent.

While I've said that there are no federal family laws, there are a couple of exceptions. The laws governing family law are state statutes, but there are two areas where the federal government gets involved. Rather than passing federal laws, which would have been constitutionally tricky, the federal government simply produced a proposed uniform statute and asked all fifty states to pass it as state law. One law governs which state has jurisdiction over a child custody case, and the other facilitates child support enforcement between states. The statute governing jurisdiction is the Uniform Child-Custody Jurisdiction and Enforcement Act (UCCJEA), and only Massachusetts has not adopted it. This law requires that before a state makes an initial determination of custody, the child must have lived in the state for a minimum of six months. The law also controls which state has jurisdiction in the case when the child moves to another state. The law was formulated to keep parents from moving from state to state to shop for more favorable custody laws. When a court makes an initial custody determination, the state where the decision was made must release its jurisdiction before any subsequent state can make a custody determination.

Sound confusing? Let me give you an example. Let's say Lenny and Jenny divorced in Texas, and Jenny has custody of their two children. Jenny moves with the children from Texas to California and lives there for two years. Lenny moves to California to be closer to his kids. Jenny starts using drugs and moves her drug-dealer boyfriend in with her and the kids. Lenny files a motion in California to change custody. The children have been in California for more than six months, but their initial custody determination was in Texas. While Texas technically still has jurisdiction, all the information about the children and their present circumstances is in California. When Lenny files for custody in California, he must notify the court of Texas's prior custody judgment. The California judge and the judge in Texas must confer to decide who should have jurisdiction. In this case, Texas will probably release jurisdiction to California after the judges confer. These UCCJEA determinations can slow down custody modifications.

Once the judge has jurisdiction, they look at many factors in deciding what is in the children's best interest. The following are a few of the factors in order of importance.

- The relationship of the children to the noncustodial parent. Is the person an integral part of the children's lives, or just a Sunday at the bowling-alley parent?
- The reason for the custodial parent's move. Judges give weight to circumstances where the custodial parent or their current spouse are moving for employment purposes. Judges reason that if a parent is moving for a better job, it will improve the children's lives, too. Likewise, if the custodial parent is moving to pursue educational opportunities. A judge may also permit a parent to move if they are moving to be closer to their family

support system, especially if the custodial parent is single or if the child has special needs. It's been my experience that judges are less inclined to approve a move simply because the custodial parent wants to remarry to someone who lives elsewhere.

When judges decide whether to grant a change in custody, they are looking at the connection the child has to the current custodial situation—not just the attachment to the parent but also the child's relationships to their community, such as school, medical providers, extracurricular activities, and extended family.

The judge must also weigh the fundamental constitutional right of the custodial parent. The U.S. Constitution has long been interpreted to protect a person's right to move houses and travel within the country freely. That protection is why you don't have to show your travel papers when crossing state borders, as citizens do in other countries.

CHILDREN'S SCHOOL

Parents sometimes disagree about schooling and seek to change custody to control school choices. Remember that person you were able to merge your parenting styles with when you were married? Well, they've gone out and gotten their own ideas since you got divorced. Your children always have attended the private school you chose together while you were married, but now, your former spouse is insisting the children attend public school. Or perhaps the children have always attended public school, but now your former spouse wants to homeschool the children. Add the lasting impact of the pandemic, and education is a hot button for many coparents. Before we get into it, let me remind you of **Rule 1**: *Whatever this shit is, it belongs to you. Don't make your shit your children's shit. Ever.*

No, the rules don't stop being rules after the divorce is final. I know it will come as a shock when I tell you some parents see the children's education as a power struggle. Let me illustrate with a story. I represented a man who had three school-aged children. The family belonged to a religion that placed a high value on stay-at-home mothers, and his former wife had homeschooled their children all of the children's lives.

When the parties divorced, they agreed to joint decision making for the children, who lived with the mother most of the time. One of the catalysts for the divorce was that my client was questioning his involvement in their church. Later, when he left the faith, he began insisting the children attend public school. When the mother refused, he came to me, demanding sole custody so he would have the power to make all the school decisions for the children.

The children's homeschool curriculum was no easy, breezy attempt at education. The family was part of a homeschool community where the curriculum was rigorous and exceeded all the state standards. Nonetheless, my client was adamant that the children needed to be in public school. It was the time for me to have a serious heart to heart with my client. I explained to him a judge was unlikely to change something that was working. His departure from their church didn't qualify as a substantial change in the children's circumstances, and it was doubtful a judge would find it was in his children's best interest that they disturb something that was working. It wasn't easy for him to accept. I suggested he hire an educational expert who was trained to evaluate children's educational needs. Her assessment revealed that, in fact, the children were above grade level in most areas. She identified some weak areas, primarily in advanced mathematics, and recommended the children take advantage of supplemental instruction offered to homeschoolers by the school district. When the mother of the children agreed, my client felt he had accomplished his goal of getting the children into some form of public school, while the mother felt she still had charge of the children's overall education. It wasn't a perfect solution for the parents, but it was a fair resolution for the children. After all, the parents' disagreement about how much influence their church had on their individual decisions wasn't the children's shit.

CHILD SUPPORT

You may have noticed that children's needs change as they grow. Anyone who's purchased shoes for a middle-school-aged boy will tell you those feet get bigger fast. Coparents need to adapt their expectations and schedules to suit their children, not the other way around. If you ask a person who divorced five years ago if they are still using the same parenting plan they started with, most will laugh. Your plan needs to change and grow with your children. Expect your plan to change permanently when the first child gets their driver's license. There can also be difficult and complex changes if a child becomes disabled or develops a severe medical condition. The hope is by the time those changes occur, you and your coparent are working so well together that you can take new developments in stride.

The toughest modifications can be those that involve money. Both child support and spousal support can be modified if there is a substantial change in either party's situation. Changes in financial circumstances are rarely easy. As a rule, the same threshold question that applies to changes in custody also applies to money modifications: there must be substantial change in circumstances. Children's needs increase with their age, the cost of living never goes down, and most people's income increases over time. Most states permit a review of child support every few years, even without proving a change in circumstances.

Whether you are reviewing child support, spousal support, or both, you will need to exchange financial information with your former spouse. You will probably be required to provide your last three pay stubs and a copy of your previous year's income tax return. I'm aware that sharing your current financial information with your former spouse feels intrusive, but it's required for both of you to prove your current income.

The modification of child support is a relatively straightforward process. Most states apply a formula and even post their calculator online. Plug in the appropriate numbers, your income, your ex's income, the number of joint and non-joint children, the number of overnights the children spend with each parent, what each parent pays for health insurance, any other unique factors, and voila! A number appears at the bottom of the form.

SPOUSAL SUPPORT

As you might expect, the modification of spousal support is more complicated. First, you must meet the threshold question of whether there has been a substantial change in circumstances. That analysis has to begin by knowing the circumstances at the time of the divorce. That's why putting all those findings in your divorce judgment pays off; all those factors that came into play then come back into play when considering whether to modify your spousal support. The most crucial consideration will be why the support was ordered in the first place and how much things have changed since then. If your attorney drafted your judgment carefully, it should be easy for a judge to compare the circumstances then and the circumstances now. Was the support awarded to compensate the receiving spouse for their contribution to the paying spouse's earning capacity, or was it awarded to maintain a lower-earning spouse's lifestyle? The judge will consider each ex-spouse's age, health, and earning potential and how those factors have changed since the divorce.

Judges don't like people who purposely reduce their income so they can reduce their support to their former spouses. Just take a look at the example from chapter 19, where a neurosurgeon left the practice of medicine and took a job selling medical equipment in an attempt to reduce his spousal support by reducing his income. It didn't work. The judge found the doctor reduced his income in bad faith, and there are consequences to bad faith. In that case, the judge continued the spousal support at the current level and required the doctor to pay all his wife's attorney fees. This example doesn't mean you can never adjust spousal support; it only means the change in circumstances must be honest. If you are paying support and you lose your job, you may be entitled to an adjustment in your support, either temporarily or permanently, depending on the circumstance.

Let's be honest; most paying spouses have a different mind-set a few years after the divorce. Perhaps the paying spouse has remarried and is now wondering why they're still sending money to someone they don't like much. Maybe their new spouse resents the spousal support they pay to their former spouse. If you are the one paying support, you may reason that your former spouse is doing just fine these days and doesn't need your money. You may even file a motion to terminate your spousal support payments. Modifications are complicated, so let's look at some possible scenarios to help illustrate.

Imagine parties who were married for five years. At the time of the divorce, the paying spouse was the Human Resources director for a major tech company and had an MBA. She made about $180,000 per year plus bonuses and stock options. The receiving spouse was a middle school teacher who had a master's degree, had been teaching for about ten years, and made about $73,000 per year when he stopped working. After they married, the spouses decided the husband would leave his teaching job and stay home with their children. The husband had also started work on a doctorate in education. The children were ages four and two at the time of the divorce. When the parties divorced, the judge ordered the wife to pay the husband transitional support for four years so he could remain at home with the children until they reached school age and have time to upgrade his teaching credentials to keep them current. The judge also awarded the husband ongoing maintenance support because of the disparity in their incomes. The wife pays $3,000 per month as transitional support for the first five years. The judge also awarded the husband an additional four years of maintenance support at a rate of $1,000 per month after the transitional support ends. Eight years of support for a five-year marriage is longer than usual, but the maintenance support was because of the significant difference in their incomes. Fast forward five years.

The children are in school full time, and the husband has finished his doctorate in education. He was hired recently as a middle school principal, and his starting salary will be $108,000. The children continue to reside primarily with the father. The wife wants the judge to terminate the husband's spousal support. She claims there have been substantial changes in the husband's circumstances; the children are now school age, and the husband has a much better job. In this instance, a judge will probably terminate the husband's spousal support. There is still a disparity in their incomes, but the children live with the father, so the wife will continue to pay child support to the husband.

Here's another scenario: The husband is a fifty-year-old machinist and is the lead supervisor for a large machine shop. He makes about $70,000 per year. He belongs to a union. The wife is a forty-eight-year-old medical laboratory technician, and she makes about $57,000 per year. Both spouses worked throughout the marriage. They have been married for twenty-three years and have one child who has just graduated college and lives independently. They have both paid into their company retirement funds and Social Security. This case a challenging call for the judge at the time of the divorce. A long-term marriage like this would call for maintenance support, but in this case, both of the spouses have reliable, living-wage jobs. Both spouses have planned for retirement, which is still quite far away. Let's assume the judge initially awarded the wife maintenance support of $500 a month for seven years in the initial divorce. Two years later, the husband was injured in an accident at work and forced to take early retirement. His income is now only $45,000 per year, from a combination of his union retirement benefits and Social Security. He filed a claim with Workers' Compensation and received a $113,000 lump sum settlement. He asks the judge to terminate the wife's spousal support. Here are a couple of questions that come to mind: Since the husband's income is now less than the wife's, could she be ordered to pay support to the husband? The answer is no. Spousal support is determined by the situation at the time of the divorce. Ex-spouses do not owe a fiduciary duty to one another. The judge has no authority to make a completely new spousal support award after a marriage is terminated by divorce. Here's another question: Does the former spouse have any claim on the husband's lump-sum disability payment? No. The answer would be different if the husband's injury occurred during the marriage, but here, where the injury happened after the divorce, she has no interest in the disability payment. The answer might be different if the husband received a large windfall, like winning the lottery, and substantially increased his income. The judge would likely terminate the wife's support in this case because the husband's income decreased because of his injury.

Here is a final example. At the time of the divorce, the forty-six-year-old husband owned an insurance agency where he was the primary agent. The agency did well, and he made about $200,000 per year. The wife was forty-three years old and had rarely worked outside the home. The couple had been married for twenty-five years. They met in college, but while the husband graduated with a business degree, the wife dropped out when she got married. After the husband graduated from college, he worked for a couple of years then returned to college to get a master's degree. While he was going to school, the wife worked as a receptionist in a dentist's office to support them. After the husband received his MBA degree and got his first job, the wife stopped working and stayed at home. Over the years, when the husband's office needed help, the wife would fill in for the administrative staff. The couple has one child, who was a freshman in college at the time of the divorce. The judge ordered the husband to pay $2,000 per month for maintenance support and $2,000 per month as compensatory support. The judge made the support obligations indefinite. Indefinite support is becoming less common, but judges still sometimes award it in long-term marriages. Here, the wife's maintenance support was intended to allow her to maintain the lifestyle she enjoyed during the marriage. The compensatory support was for the wife's contributions to the husband's earning capacity and business. Five years after the divorce, the wife remarries. Her new husband is exceptionally wealthy, and the wife no longer needs the husband's support to maintain the lifestyle she enjoyed during their marriage. The husband files a motion to terminate the wife's support.

What do you suppose happens? The outcome could vary depending on the jurisdiction. The outlook on spousal support has changed along with opinions around gender roles. It's possible a judge would terminate the wife's maintenance support because the need for support to maintain the wife's lifestyle no longer exists. Others might find her maintenance support was based on the situation at the time of the divorce, and the wife's income has not changed. Her new husband's income and the lifestyle the wife enjoys with him should not be considered. The compensatory support should continue because the wife earned it due to her support of the first husband's education and business.

CONTEMPT OF COURT

Clients often ask, "What do you do when your former spouse won't do what the divorce judgment orders?" Police will not enforce your divorce judgment or your parenting plan. In fact, they get grumpy when someone calls them because the caller was supposed to pick up their child at 6 p.m., and it's now 6:15, and no one is answering the door. When a person violates a court order, your recourse is to file a motion to hold them in contempt of court for not obeying the judge's orders.

There are two types of contempt actions. The first is remedial contempt, and it's a move requested to remedy the noncompliance. As an example, you file a motion to modify your child support, and before a judge can review support, both of you must produce records to prove your income. You produce your pay stubs and income tax records, but your former spouse does not. Now what? Your attorney sends your former spouse a discovery request and gives them a deadline to produce the information. The deadline passes, and your lawyer files a motion to compel the production of those records. The judge orders your ex to produce the information within five days, and your ex ignores the deadline. Your lawyer files a motion to hold your ex in contempt of court for defying the judge's order. The process takes time. Your lawyer can file a motion for remedial contempt meant to remedy your ex's contempt. The judge can order your ex to pay a whopping fine for every day they don't produce the documents and can order your ex to pay all your legal fees associated with trying to get your ex to cough up the information.

Second, there's something called punitive contempt. It's when you ask the judge to punish your ex by putting him or her in jail until they comply. The upside? Your ex is in jail. (You know you fantasize about it.) The downside? Your ex may be entitled to a court-appointed lawyer to help with the contempt charges. If you are dealing with someone who is unrepresented, it might be an advantage that you don't want to give them.

There are times when contempt of a judge's order can lead to a modification. Say you have a court-ordered parenting plan, but every time you go to pick up your child, your ex isn't there. It goes on for months. Your lawyer files a remedial contempt action, and the judge orders your ex to comply. The next time you go to pick up your child, the house is empty, and your ex has moved. Your lawyer files a punitive contempt action, but you should also be filing a motion to change custody. Although there may not be a significant change in either spouse's circumstances in most jurisdictions, intentional and systematic denial of parenting time is grounds to change custody to the parent who is more willing to foster a relationship with the noncustodial parent.

That said, here's a reality check: contempt charges won't make your ex a nicer person or a better parent, and they won't stop your ex from being a colossal waste of space. Contempt charges can't create money and can prolong a case and make it more hostile.

Part III

ENDINGS AND BEGINNINGS

Y ou've made it through the shock, the sadness, and all the times you thought your divorce would never end. Your divorce is final— now what?

21

REGRETS, DATING, AND THE NEW WOMAN OR MAN

We are social animals, and we long for connection, but after the way your last relationship ended, sometimes you may not be sure how to connect in a healthy way. Remember **Rule 7**: *You're impaired. Don't do stupid shit you'll regret later.* You may not think you are still impaired, but trust me, a year from now, you'll look back and shake your head at how "out of it" you were. Here is my advice:

- Go out with friends and have fun, but don't date anyone exclusively until you regularly work with a therapist—and preferably not at all for the first year.
- Do not involve your children in your social life.
- Do not introduce your children or your former spouse to a new person unless you are damn sure they are sticking around for the long haul.
- Do not involve yourself financially with a new partner unless and until you are engaged. And don't get engaged until at least a year after your divorce.
- If your new partner is in a big hurry, pump the brakes.

Most people who divorce go on to new partners. For some, it takes years; for others, just a minute. Either way, coping with your feelings around this will be hard.

Along with the bundle of rights and responsibilities you get when you marry, you also develop a set of expectations for the future. You expect that you will experience life's events with your spouse; that you'll attend your children's school, church, and sporting events; and that you'll mark their milestones together. Divorce destroys those expectations.

If you are wise, you will spend some time with a licensed therapist working through the feelings about those dashed expectations.

WHEN YOU'RE DATING OR YOUR EX IS DATING

Nothing says, "it's over," like learning your former spouse has a new partner. It's coming, so brace yourself. Hopefully, you will have discussed the possibility with your therapist and worked through your feelings in advance, but regardless of how prepared you are, it will sting. You will still wonder, "What's the new person got that I don't have?"

If you think it's hard to think about your former spouse with someone else, think about how your kids feel. Children don't understand that dating is like trying on shoes. Unlike riding a bicycle, dating is something you can forget how to do when you've been married a while, and it's going to take some practice to get your groove back. You will undoubtedly date a few people while relearning the process only to discover they're not the one for you. In fact, I hope you date a lot of new people before you find a person you want to be with, and I hope that, until you find the shoe that fits, you keep that part of your life private from both your children and your former spouse.

You most certainly should have a social life, and you may tell your children you are going out with friends, and but until you believe a new person is someone you want in your life permanently, please don't introduce them to your children. When you introduce children to a new person, that person will naturally be on their best behavior; they will want your kids to like them. Your children may attach easily. Even teenagers may become attached to your new love interest. Your kids won't understand when you explain you don't see Bambi anymore because it just didn't feel right; it felt right to them.

Before you introduce your new partner to your children, observe **Rule 8**: *Don't blindside your ex-spouse*. And let your former spouse know. This step is critical if you are serious about rebuilding a trusting coparenting relationship, so observe the golden rule and "do unto others as you would have them do unto you." Your children are your ex's children, too, and whenever possible, you should decide together what is best for them. Now, I know what you're thinking: discussing your new love with your old love is out of the question. You're right; I'm not suggesting you have a long discussion about your new love's strengths and weaknesses or how he or she can bench two hundred pounds. I am suggesting, at a minimum, that you tell your ex-spouse you are dating someone before your ex sees it on Facebook, or worse, hears it from your children. Before the children meet the new love, think how you will introduce this new person; be intentional and thoughtful, even if your former spouse isn't.

Do not show up at soccer practice unannounced with Dirk because you know it will make your former spouse crazy; revenge always rebounds double on your children. There are therapists, mediators, and parenting-time coordinators who specialize in facilitating discussions around parenting time and boundaries. If you feel you are close to making your new relationship permanent, consider inviting your former spouse to meet with you and a facilitator to discuss guidelines.

As you get to know someone new, you will inevitably discuss your former marriage and your children. You want that person to like you and to see potential in your relationship. It's tempting to tell the new person the divorce was all your ex's fault because your ex is an evil person. It's also tempting to report that it's your ex's fault you don't have a better relationship with your kids. You and I both know the truth is much more complicated and nuanced. You might tell them those half-truths for several reasons. Certainly, you don't want this new person to think you are a bad parent or that they are taking a risk getting involved with you. Admitting to someone you hope to have a relationship with that you bear some responsibility for the demise of your last serious relationship or that you have a part to play in the distance you feel with your children may feel like the kiss of death. It's important to be honest—and accountable. You don't want your new love jumping in to defend you if they feel you are being wronged when the truth is more complicated.

The temptation to protect ourselves by shading the truth is a very human tendency. It may have even been a problem in your former marriage. Experts tell us that the best relationships are born out of honesty. That means fighting the natural temptation to protect yourself by omitting or manipulating the truth. This fresh start is the perfect place to work through those issues with a therapist and commit to honesty in any new relationship. See why it's important not to rush into a new relationship? You know that, with time, your new love is going to discover your strengths and weaknesses anyway, but by then, the dishonesty damage may have already been done to your new relationship as well as your relationship with your coparent and your children. Failing to be honest in the beginning can set up a conflict that may never go away and was entirely avoidable. Start a new relationship the way you hope it will go on. Be honest, accept responsibility for your part, and prioritize your children.

STEPPARENTING ON THE NEW FRONTIER

No relationship is more emotionally charged than that of a stepparent. I've had one, I've been one, and I've counseled hundreds of them, so let's get a few things straight.

- Your new love is not the parent. Don't try to make them the parent, even if they want the job and it makes life easier for you.
- Your new love should not fight your battles or take over communication with your coparent.
- Your new spouse should be supportive of your role as the parent, should never express an opinion about your coparent in front of or within ear shot of your children, and should never countermand decisions made by you or your coparent.
- Your new spouse's role is to be a bonus in your children's lives, not an obstacle to them spending time with you.
- Your new spouse (and you) should treat all children, theirs and yours, with the same respect and care.

We're all going to make our own mistakes, some new and some repeats. A famous quote that likely came from Al-Anon, but which is frequently misattributed to Albert Einstein, says, "the definition of insanity is doing the same thing over and over again and expecting a different result." We can't stop making the same mistakes until we understand that they were mistakes and that we have the power to change them. Ensuring that you aren't just making the same choices over and over while expecting a different result requires self-examination and evaluation. It's uncomfortable, and no one likes it. Do it anyway. You can do it with the help of a therapist, or self-help books, or journaling. The important thing is that you do it. Just as regular exercise will help you live longer, regular self-reflection will help you find and maintain relationships that live longer.

This reasoning also applies to your relationship with your children. Children will seek their own level with each parent, depending on what both you and your child find comfortable. If you are satisfied with a relationship that remains polite and superficial, your children will accept it and move on to others who are more emotionally available. If you want a deep, enduring relationship with your children, you have to build it. It's important to remember that the time you spend raising your children is only a tiny fraction of the time you will spend relating to them as adults.

22

DRUNK DIALING AND WORSE

Just as you will inevitably stalk your ex online, it's also inevitable you'll have second thoughts. After all, you entered this relationship with hope and optimism and devoted a lot of time to making it work. It's likely no one knows you as well as the person you are divorcing, and endings are hard.

The day may come when you are sitting at home feeling lonely, with only a bottle of chardonnay for company, watching Hallmark movies, or scrolling through the photos on your phone, and before you know it, you've dialed their number. I've known clients who were determined to make a clean break and clients who lingered in the waiting room for a long while. I even know of clients who were still occasionally hooking up with their exes years later. It's a little like quitting smoking. For some people, the only way is cold turkey. For others, the gradual way works best, and for some, they're still sneaking the occasional cigarette years later.

If you and your spouse decide to reconcile, there are important considerations. Some reconciling couples go so far as to sign an agreement about how they will navigate their reconciliation. If your divorce is final, this agreement would be considered a prenuptial agreement that would lay out how you would handle it if the reconciliation and remarriage don't work out. If, however, your divorce was not finalized before you reconcile, the agreement is considered a postnuptial agreement. Postnuptial agreements are much less enforceable than prenuptial agreements. The reason is that pesky bundle of rights and responsibilities we keep talking about, including the fiduciary duty one spouse owes another. Judges reason if one spouse owes a duty of loyalty and fair dealing to the other spouse, a postnuptial agreement may violate that duty if the agreement favors one spouse over the other. There are many purposes for a postnuptial agreement. The agreements may guide how assets will be recombined or later divided if necessary and whether spousal support will be awarded. Some agreements also cover what happens if a spouse dies. In most states, postnuptial contracts can't determine custody, parenting time, or child support.

As you look forward to a future without your former spouse, it's natural to have doubts; sometimes it's just fear talking—fear of the unknown and fear of change—and this is where therapy can help. Still, it's also possible you reach this point and decide it's worth another try. If that happens, try to remember that the issues that brought you to this point are probably not gone. If you're going to give your relationship another try, give it the best chance of success. Start by making couples therapy a condition of your reconciliation. If you've already reached the point where all your assets have been divided, don't rush to recombine them. Take your time and date each other. Insist on courting, just like it was the beginning of your relationship—because it is. This phase should include couples counseling because lasting change is rare and hard.

23

MOVING ON

While you won't believe it at the beginning of your divorce, you can learn and grow from the experience.

I want to tell you the story of one of my dearest clients. She was involved in a criminal matter and not a divorce, but the lesson she taught me is worth sharing. Throughout my career, I also practiced criminal law as a public defender. The overlap isn't unusual, especially in smaller communities. I first met Nina when I was appointed to represent her on some serious criminal charges. Nina had a host of problems; she was addicted to methamphetamine, working as an exotic dancer, and associating with some very bad people. One night, she and a couple of associates stopped by a local convenience store. While Nina stayed in the car, acting as lookout and getaway driver, the two men she was with robbed the store at gunpoint. I first met her in jail, detoxing and facing charges for armed robbery.

To say Nina was angry was an understatement. She demanded I get her out of jail immediately and informed me she could *not* go to prison. The law, however, had a different opinion. Armed robbery carried a mandatory five-year prison sentence in our state. If convicted, Nina would not be eligible for any treatment or training programs while in prison and would not earn any time off her sentence for good behavior. A friend of hers posted her bail so she could get out of jail for a few weeks. However, things got worse during that time when the child welfare agency removed her young son and put him in foster care. Over the next few weeks, Nina and I had some difficult conversations. While I was able to negotiate a better possible sentence for her, there was no way to make the specter of prison go away. I'm a lawyer, not a magician. I was able to negotiate her case out of the mandatory sentencing requirement and get her a three-year prison sentence with the possibility of early release if she became involved in the in-house drug treatment program the prison offered. Not surprisingly, Nina didn't see this as great progress. I reminded her the three years were going to pass anyway, and the only question was whether she would come out of prison better or bitter.

Ultimately, Nina pled guilty to the lesser charges and got the three-year sentence we had negotiated. I remained in touch with Nina throughout her prison sentence because I also represented her in the foster care case involving her son. Then Nina did something amazing. She signed up for every prison course, class, and program she could get into. She earned her high school diploma, took some college courses, learned to be a barista, and gained several other valuable work skills. She joined therapy groups and got into the drug treatment program as soon as she was eligible. She was so successful in the program that she cut her sentence by nearly a year and earned an early furlough. While on parole, she enrolled in community college and graduated two years later with an associate's degree in accounting. When she had trouble finding a job because of her felony conviction, she started her own business. Ten years later, we are still in touch; Nina is flourishing and dedicated to helping other people thrive after prison.

I share this story to illustrate that you can accomplish much more than you think with the right mind-set. If you're prepared to see your divorce as an opportunity and not a tragedy, you will learn and grow. Sometimes people accomplish this on their own, through study and self-reflection, and sometimes they need help from a professional therapist. Learning from your experience and not making the same mistakes takes work.

When you divorce, you not only lose the future you had planned but also you often lose other people you love, like your former spouse's family. If you are lucky, you will find a way to remain close to those family members, but you may have to accept it's not always possible. A client once told me her mother cut her former husband out of every family photograph, even her wedding pictures! You may lose friends. It could be because your friends have aligned with your former spouse, or it may just be they don't want to be involved with your divorce. I also think sometimes it's because they worry divorce might be catching. Either way, these secondary losses are painful.

I once had a client who called me several weeks after her divorce was final to invite me to lunch. When I joined her at the restaurant, she said she just wanted me to see her when she wasn't temporarily insane. She also told me she had decided that before she got serious about anyone again, she intended to introduce them to her accountant and her lawyer because she trusted our judgment. She did remarry, and I helped her with her side of a prenuptial agreement and a new will after the wedding. I see them on social media, and they're still together.

Once you've fought through the sadness, the guilt, and the feelings of failure, you'll come out stronger and more self-aware. You've worked hard on becoming whole; don't make the mistake of settling for someone who hasn't done that work. You deserve someone who brings a whole person to the party. Marriage after divorce can be complicated. When you marry the first time, it's often the case that neither of you has a lot of assets, and you set about building a life together. But when you marry after a divorce, the situation is different; you have assets, and you may have children. This book isn't about those issues, but I urge you to find and read those books, take your time, cultivate an attitude of curiosity and a little healthy skepticism and get to know yourself first.

The greatest gifts you can give yourself are not settling or selling yourself short and giving yourself time to heal and reflect. Take a look at the titles I've suggested in appendix A at the end of this book. I highly recommend the work of Dr. Brené Brown, and in particular, her book *Daring Greatly*. Dr. Brown has a favorite quote excerpted from a speech by Theodore Roosevelt. It seems like a perfect place to end.

As my French grandmother would have said, "J'espère que vous en tirerez une bénédiction," which means, *I hope you get a blessing from it.*

It is not the critic who counts; not the man who points out how the strong man stumbles, or where the doer of deeds could have done them better. The credit belongs to the man who is actually in the arena, whose face is marred by dust and sweat and blood; who strives valiantly; who errs, who comes short again and again, because there is no effort without error and shortcoming; but who does actually strive to do the deeds; who knows great enthusiasms, the great devotions; who spends himself in worthy cause; who at best knows in the end the triumph of great achievement, and who at worst, if he fails, at least fails while daring greatly, so that his place shall never be with those cold and timid souls who neither know victory nor defeat.[1]

Appendix A

RESOURCES

BOOKS FOR ADULTS

Codependent No More by Melodie Beattie
Daring Greatly by Brené Brown
The Gifts of Imperfection by Brené Brown
The Parent's Guide to Birdnesting: A Child-Centered Approach to Parenting during Separation and Divorce by Ann Gold Buscho, PhD
Parenting with Love and Logic by Foster W. Cline and Jim Fay
Joint Custody with a Jerk by Judy Corcoran and Julie Ross
No Break Up Can Break You: The Definitive Recovery Guide for Men by Nick Dawson
Untamed by Glennon Doyle
Splitting: Protecting Yourself While Divorcing Someone with Borderline or Narcissistic Personality Disorder by Bill Eddy and Randy Kreger
Too Good to Leave, Too Bad to Stay by Mira Kirshenbaum
The Dance of Anger: A Woman's Guide to Changing the Patterns of Intimate Relationships by Harriet Lerner, PhD
Saving Your Second Marriage before It Starts by Dr. Les Parrott and Dr. Leslie Parrott
High Conflict: Why We Get Trapped and How We Get Out by Amanda Ripley
Crazy Time by Abigail Trafford
And, finally, anything by David Sedaris or Jenny Lawson because you need a good laugh.

BOOKS FOR CHILDREN

Dinosaurs Divorce by Marc Brown
Susie and the Dandelions by Ana Cybela

The Invisible String by Patrice Karst
What to Do When You Don't Want to Be Apart by Kristen Lavallee, PhD, and
     Dr. Silvia Schneider
Two Homes by Claire Masurel
The Kissing Hand by Audrey Penn
The List of Things That Will Not Change by Rebecca Stead

COPARENTING APPS

New apps are being developed all the time to help families manage
schedules and communicate better; these are a few of the most popular.
Some are free, and some require a subscription.

Coparently
Cozi
Custody Connection
Google Calendar
Ourfamilywizard
2houses.com
WeParent

YOUTUBE CHANNELS AND PODCASTS

Love and Logic YouTube channel hosted by Dr. Charles Fay of the Love and
     Logic Institute.
The Love and Logic Podcast hosted by Dr. Charles Fay and Jedd Hafer

Appendix B

SAMPLE DOCUMENTS

The following documents are provided here as examples only. They are not intended to substitute for documents prepared by a qualified lawyer after careful consideration of your individual issues.

SAMPLE RETAINER AGREEMENT

I, _____ (client) hereby retain the law office of _____ ("The Attorney") to represent me regarding: _____ (Type of Matter)

1. I agree to pay The Attorney a retainer in the amount of $_____. I understand The Attorney has not accepted my case and will not act as my Attorney until I have signed this agreement and paid the retainer. Any unearned portion of the retainer will be returned to me at the end of my case, even though the retainer may have been deposited on my behalf by a third party.

2. I agree to pay The Attorney at a rate of $_____ per hour for work performed by The Attorney.

3. I understand fees and costs will be billed monthly and that any balance owing is due and payable ten (10) days from the date of the monthly statement. If I have authorized credit card payment, The Attorney will charge any unpaid balance to my credit card at the end of each billing cycle. The Attorney may cease to provide

further legal services if I fail to pay all charges in full each month. I understand a late payment penalty of ___% percent per month will be charged on all unpaid balances over 30 days old. I further understand that The Attorney will withdraw from my case if my unpaid balance exceeds $_____ for more than 30 days.

4. The Attorney may withdraw and apply my retainer and any other sums in my trust account to my bill at any time unless I give The Attorney specific written instructions to the contrary. If there are sums remaining in my trust account to be refunded, they will be refunded to me during the next regular monthly billing cycle.

5. The Attorney will tell me if it becomes necessary to deposit additional sums in The Attorney's trust account to cover projected future fees and costs. I will promptly deposit the requested sum with The Attorney. The Attorney will have the right to cease all work on my behalf if such additional sums are not promptly deposited with The Attorney. I understand that The Attorney will not proceed to trial on my behalf unless there is a minimum balance of $_____ in my trust account ____ days before trial.

6. I understand and agree The Attorney may assign all or any portion of the work to be performed to another attorney or others working under The Attorney's supervision and charge me for the service.

7. I agree to pay to The Attorney, in addition to any fee charged, all out-of-pocket costs incurred by The Attorney on my behalf or in connection with my case. I understand costs may include such things as filing and trial fees, photocopy charges, long-distance telephone charges, long distance facsimile expenses, service fees, appraisal fees, investigation and deposition costs, court reporter fees, custody evaluation fees, arbitrator and witness fees, and any other costs deemed necessary by The Attorney. I understand I am liable for all fees charged by other professionals for work on my case. I will pay those fees as agreed, and The Attorney is not responsible as my agent for those fees.

8. I hereby grant The Attorney a lien against any sums held for me in The Attorney's trust account and against any money or property (including land) received by me or money judgments

entered in my favor in this or any other legal proceeding. The lien will be removed only when my bill is paid in full. I specifically authorize The Attorney to receive any said funds or property and to pay themself all fees and costs from said funds and property before releasing the balance to me.

9. I understand The Attorney will use their best effort in representing me. The Attorney has given me no assurances about the outcome of matters being handled by The Attorney except that it is impossible to determine in advance the amount of time needed to complete my case. I acknowledge The Attorney's average fee for one day of trial is $_____ and $_____ for each day of trial preparation. The Attorney's actual fee may be less or more than these amounts.

10. I understand that it is not the responsibility of my spouse or any other person to pay my attorney fees and costs, even though The Attorney may ask the court to order my spouse to pay part or all of my attorney fees and costs. The responsibility to pay my fees and costs is mine. I know awards of fees by the court are unpredictable and that it is I who have hired and must pay The Attorney.

11. I agree to fully cooperate with The Attorney and others working on my case. I will keep The Attorney advised of all matters which may have a bearing on my case, be truthful with The Attorney at all times, follow through with all agreements made with The Attorney, keep appointments, give depositions, produce documents, respond promptly to The Attorney's letters, appear for scheduled court appearances, and keep The Attorney informed of any change of my address or telephone number or employment within five days of the change. If I fail to appear at any given court hearing or trial, I authorize The Attorney to exercise discretion and proceed in whatever manner The Attorney sees fit.

12. I agree that The Attorney is not required to complete work on my case and that they may withdraw as my attorney at any time if I fail to comply with the exact terms of this agreement. I understand The Attorney will send written notice of intent

to withdraw to my last known address and need give me no other notice.

13. I agree the prevailing party shall be entitled to recover collection costs and attorney fees incurred in the trial and the appeal of any suit or action filed to enforce the provisions of this agreement, including any arbitration hearing. The prevailing party shall also be allowed to recover as part of any judgment a sum sufficient to pay the prevailing party for any attorney fees which may be incurred after entry of judgment to collect said judgment from the non-prevailing party. Any lawsuit filed to enforce this agreement will be filed in (county and state) _____.

14. I understand and agree that if I request The Attorney to perform services on any other legal matter after the signing of this agreement, the terms of this agreement shall apply to and be binding in the new matters until a new fee agreement is negotiated between The Attorney and me.

15. I acknowledge that failure of The Attorney at any time to require strict performance of any provision of this agreement shall not limit The Attorney's right to enforce the provision, nor shall any waiver by The Attorney of any breach of any provision be a waiver of or prejudice The Attorney's right otherwise to demand strict performance of the provision or any other provision of this agreement.

16. I acknowledge I am free to review this agreement with another attorney before signing it.

I HAVE READ THIS AGREEMENT, HAVE RECEIVED A COPY OF IT, AND AGREE TO THE TERMS AND CONDITIONS AS STATED. THERE ARE NO VERBAL AGREEMENTS BETWEEN CLIENT AND THE ATTORNEY MODIFYING OR EXPANDING THE TERMS OF THIS AGREEMENT.

BUDGET WORKSHEET

The following worksheet is similar to what the court will require if you
intend to ask for child or spousal support. The court will likely require
that you attach a few recent pay stubs and your tax return for the most
recent year to any statement of income and expenses.

1. Sources of income

Wages/Salary: *(monthly, before taxes)*	
$_____ *per hour*	_____*hours/week*
	Subtotal A: $_____

(Complete table below with monthly averages, before taxes. Explain "other" amounts)

Tips:	$	Bonuses/Commission:	$
Workers Comp:	$	Interest:	$
Social Security:	$	Annuity:	$
Unemployment:	$	Trust:	$
Disability:	$	Dividends:	$
TANF:	$	Other:	$
Other:	$	Other:	$
Other:	$	Other:	$
Expense reimbursement/per diem allowance that reduces personal living expenses: $			
		Subtotal B: $_____	

Gross monthly income TOTAL *(add Subtotals A + B)* $_____

2. Spousal/partner support

    a. Received by me *(from anyone)* $_____
    b. Paid by me *(to anyone)* $_____

3. Health insurance

a. Premium to cover just me $_____
b. Premium paid for joint children $_____
c. Out of pocket medical costs paid for joint children $_____
d. Subsidies received for health insurance costs $_____
e. Public health insurance   ☐ yes   ☐ no

4. Other

a. Union dues $_____

b. Social Security or Veteran's Benefits received for $_____
   children

   i. Person with disability is: ☐ child   ☐ me   ☐ other parent

c. Childcare expenses for joint children (12 or younger) $_____

   i. Does anyone else share the cost of childcare?   ☐ yes ☐ no

     1. Name: _____   Amount: $_____

1. Fixed Costs

Description	*Monthly Amount*
A. RESIDENCE:	
Mortgage or Rent	
Second Mortgage/Home Equity Loan	
Property Taxes and Insurance (if not included in mortgage)	
B. UTILITIES: *(averaged over the year)*	
Electricity	
Gas	
Water/Sewer	
Trash/Recycling	
Telephone/Cell Phone	
Cable/Internet	
C. TRANSPORTATION:	
Car Payments	
Fuel	
Bus pass/Van pool/Etc.	
Other (specify):	
D. INSURANCE:	
Life	
Automobile	
Medical/Dental	
Other (specify):	
E. Food and Household Items	
F. Unreimbursed health costs, including medications	
G. Court/Agency-Ordered Support Payments in other cases	

TOTAL FIXED COSTS:

2. Debts

Name of Creditor (who debt is owed to)	Balance Due	Monthly Payment
Total Monthly Debt Payments:		

Total Fixed Costs + Monthly Debts = \$_____

This is only a sample to be used for demonstrative purposes. It contains some possible suggested wording of a typical divorce petition. Every state is different, no two divorces are alike, and your judgment may look very different. This sample is only provided to suggest provisions you may want to discuss with your attorney. It is not intended to replace advice from an experienced licensed family law attorney.

STATE OF _____

IN THE COUNTY OF _____

Family Court Division

John Doe,	)	Case Number
Petitioner	)	
	)	Petition for Dissolution of Marriage
	)	
Mary Doe,	)	With Minor Children and Support
Respondent	)	
	)	

Petitioner hereby petitions the court for a judgment of dissolution of marriage.

Petitioner alleges:

    1. Petitioner is a resident of the state of _____ and has been for the _____ months prior to this petition being filed.

    2. Petitioner is a resident of the state of _____ and has been for the _____ months prior to this petition being filed.

3. Respondent is a resident of the state of _____ and has been for the _____ months prior to this petition being filed.

4. Petitioner and Respondent were married on _____ (date) in _____ (city and county) and have continuously been husband and wife since.

5. Irreconcilable differences have caused the irremediable breakdown of the marriage.

6. Petitioner and Respondent have _____ children born of this marriage, _____ _____ (list names and ages). Petitioner/ Respondent should be awarded sole legal custody subject to Respondent/Petitioner's right to reasonable and regularly parenting time. OR The parties are both fit and proper parents and should be awarded joint legal custody of the children and awarded reasonable and regular parenting time.

7. Petitioner/Respondent should be awarded reasonable child support and spousal support.

8. The parties own certain real property that should be divided equitably.

9. The parties own certain personal property, including bank accounts and retirement fund that should be divided equitably.

10. The parties have certain debts which should be divided equally between them.

11. Petitioner/Respondent should be responsible to pay Respondent/Petitioner's reasonable attorney fees and costs. OR Each party should pay their own attorney fees. If this matter becomes contested the court may determine the just and proper division of attorney fees.

Your petition could look much different. Many states now use a standard form with checked boxes and fill-in blanks.

This form is only a sample to be used for demonstrative purposes. It contains some possible suggested wording of a typical motion. Every state is different, no two divorces are alike, and your order may look very different. This sample is only provided to suggest provisions you may want to discuss with your attorney. It is not intended to replace advice from an experienced licensed family law attorney.

STATE OF _____
IN THE COUNTY OF _____
Family Court Division

John Doe, Petitioner	)))	Case Number
	)	Temporary Protective Order of Restraint, Children
	)	
Mary Doe, Respondent	)))	(Pre-Judgment Status Quo)

_____

Based on the motion and affidavit filed herein, the request for a Status Quo Order is hereby: _____ Allowed _____ Denied. (check one).

IT IS HEREBY ORDERED that until further order of the court,
Petitioner and Respondent are both restrained from: Changing the
minor child(ren)'s usual place of residence and from interfering with
the present placement of the minor child(ren) from interfering with the
present placement and daily schedule of the child(ren), from interfering
with the other parent's usual contact and parenting time with the child,
or from taking the child out of the state without the written permission
of the other parent or permission of the court; or in any manner disturb-
ing the current schedule and daily routine of the child(ren) until custody
and parenting time have been determined.

The names and age(s) of the minor child(ren) is/are:

_____

_____

_____.

**Your order could look much different. Many states now use a
standard form with checked boxes and fill-in blanks.**

This form is only a sample to be used for demonstrative purposes. It contains some possible suggested wording of a typical motion. Every state is different, no two divorces are alike, and your order may look very different. This sample is only provided to suggest provisions you may want to discuss with your attorney. It is not intended to replace advice from an experienced licensed family law attorney.

STATE OF _____

IN THE COUNTY OF _____

Family Court Division

John Doe,	)	Case Number
Petitioner	)	
	)	Temporary Protective Order of Restraint, Financial
	)	
Mary Doe,	)	(Pre-Judgment Status Quo)
Respondent	)	
	)	

Based on the motion and affidavit filed herein, the request for a Status Quo Order is hereby: _____ Allowed _____ Denied. (check one).

IT IS HEREBY ORDERED that until further order of the court,

1. Petitioner and Respondent are both restrained from:
   a. Cancelling, modifying, terminating or allowing to lapse for nonpayment of premiums any policy of life insurance, health

insurance, homeowners or renter insurance or automobile insurance that one party maintains to provide coverage for the other party or a minor child of the parties or any life insurance policy that name either of the parties or a minor child of the parties as a beneficiary.

b. Cancelling, modifying, terminating or allowing to lapse for nonpayment cellular telephone service that one party maintains for the other party or a minor child of the parties.

c. Changing beneficiaries or covered parties under any policy of life insurance, health insurance, homeowner or renter insurance or automobile insurance that one party maintains to provide coverage for the other party or a minor child of the parties.

d. Transferring, encumbering, concealing or disposing of property in which the other party has an interest, in any manner, without written consent of the other party or an order of the court except in the usual course of business or for necessities of life.

This order does not restrict the payment by either party of:

1. Attorney fees in this action.
2. Real estate and income taxes.
3. Mental health therapy for either party or a minor child of the parties.
4. Expenses necessary to provide for the safety and welfare of a party or a minor child of the parties.

Your order could look much different. Many states now use a standard form with checked boxes and fill-in blanks.

This form is only a sample to be used for demonstrative purposes. It contains some possible suggested wording of a typical divorce judgment. Every state is different, no two divorces are alike, and your Judgment may look very different. This sample is only provided to suggest provisions you may want to discuss with your attorney. It is not intended to replace advice from an experienced licensed family law attorney.

STATE OF _____

IN THE COUNTY OF _____

Family Court Division

John Doe,	)	Case Number
Petitioner	)	
	)	Judgment of Dissolution of
		Marriage
	)	
Mary Doe,	)	With Minor Children
Respondent	)	Includes Money Judgments
	)	

This Matter came before the court on the Petition of John Doe for the dissolution of his marriage to Respondent, Mary Doe.

The parties have reached an agreement on all matters pertaining to their children, debts, and marital estate. OR The court has heard testimony and received exhibits and been fully informed as to the issues and makes the following decisions regarding the parties' children debts and marital estate.

Findings of Fact: (it is important to include this information because it recites the current circumstances and may form the basis of any future modifications).

1. The marital relationship has irretrievably broken, and the parties have irreconcilable differences. (If you have entered into a covenant marriage in one of the three states that permit them, you will have a finding of fault here.) (If you live in a state that permits alternative filings alleging fault, you will have a finding of fault here.)

2. The parties reside in _____ (county) _____ (state) and have done so for the past _____ (months/years), thereby meeting the requirements for residency required by state statute.

3. The parties were married on _____ (date) in _____ (county and state). The parties separated on _____ (date).

4. The parties have ___(#)___ of joint minor children. The parties have ___(#)___ children between the ages of 18 and 21. Husband has ___(#)___ non-joint minor children, and Wife has ___(#)___, non-joint minor children.

5. Petitioner and Respondent are the following children's legal parents: _____ _____ (list names and ages) and have a duty to support these children.

6. The determination of custody and parenting time in this Judgment is in the best interest of the minor children.

7. Petitioner is/is not now pregnant, and Respondent is/is not the unborn child's parent.

8. Respondent is/is not now pregnant, and Petitioner is/is not the unborn child's parent.

9. Husband is employed full time/part time as a _____ at _____. His monthly income from all sources is $_____. He pays $_____ per month for the children's health insurance and $_____ per month for his own health insurance. Husband does/does not have a Health Savings Account.

10. Wife is employed full time/part time as a _____ at _____. Her monthly income from all sources is $_____. She pays $_____ per month for the children's health insurance and $_____ per month for her own health insurance. Wife does/does not have a Health Savings Account.

11. Husband/Wife receives $_____ per month in social security/veteran's benefits.
12. Husband/Wife receives $_____ per month from Wife/Husband as spousal support.
13. Husband/Wife pays $_____ per month dues to a labor union or other mandatory professional organization.
14. The cost of work-related childcare for the parties' joint children is $_____.
15. Husband incurs the following extraordinary expense for the children (include special education, tutoring, special medical needs, long-distance travel for parenting time).
16. Husband incurs the following extraordinary expense for the children (include special education, tutoring, special medical needs, long-distance travel for parenting time).
17. Husband's education and training includes: _____

   _____ (list degrees and licenses).
18. Wife's education and training includes: _____

   _____ (list degrees and licenses).
19. Husband's health is (good, fair, poor, list circumstances that could impact his ability to work).
20. Wife's health is (good, fair, poor, list circumstances that could impact her ability to work).
21. Husband/Wife has been absent from the workforce for _____ years for the purpose of remaining at home to care for the minor children.
22. Husband/Wife contributed to Wife/Husband obtaining a professional degree in _____, by working and supporting the family during Wife/Husband's professional education and is entitled to compensatory spousal support.
23. No evidence of domestic violence was offered, and the court makes no finding regarding domestic violence. OR Neither parent has a history of committing domestic violence. OR Petitioner/Respondent has a history of domestic violence, and the statutory presumption against custody is overcome.

24. Petitioner/Respondent has been convicted of Driving Under the Influence of Intoxicants in the past 12 months, and sufficient safeguard had been included in the parenting plan to protect the minor children. OR Neither party has been convicted of Driving Under the Influence of Intoxicants in the past 12 months.

Orders of the Court:

1. The marriage of the parties is hereby dissolved. (Some states have waiting periods. That information would be inserted here.)
2. Husband/Wife is restored to their former name of _____.
3. Wills, Trusts, and Life Insurance.
   a. Any provision of a party's will that is now in force that benefits the now-former spouse is revoked, and the will shall be interpreted as if the former spouse did not survive the testator.
   b. Any provision in any trust created by or for the benefit of a party that is now in force that benefits the now-former spouse will be deemed revoked, and the trust will be interpreted as if the former spouse did not survive the decedent. The intent of this provision is to prevent the former spouse from having any involvement in the trust in any capacity, including as a trustee or a beneficiary.
   c. Except as otherwise ordered in this Judgment, any designation of the now-former spouse as a beneficiary of any benefit, including, but not limited to retirement benefits, IRA accounts, life insurance policies, annuities, or other asset where a party can designate a beneficiary to receive proceeds of that asset upon the death of that party, that was in place on or before the date of this Judgment are deemed to have been revoked. The benefit will be paid to the secondary or contingent beneficiary, or if no beneficiary is named, then to the decedent's estate. The surviving spouse will cooperate with the decedent's estate in assuring this directive is completed, specifically including the affirmative responsibility to disclaim

in writing and within six months of the date of the death to assure that the surviving former spouse does not receive any benefit as a result of the decedent's failure to modify the beneficiary designation of the above-described assets.

4. Custody.

   a. The parties are both fit and proper parents and are awarded joint legal custody of the parties' minor children OR Husband/Wife is awarded sole legal custody of and decision-making authority for the parties' minor children.

   b. The parties will share time with their minor children according to the attached parenting plan identified herein as Exhibit 1.

   c. Husband/Wife will pay to Wife/Husband the sum of $_____ per month as child support. (Include specifics if your state is one that awards support per child rather than in the aggregate.)

   d. As additional support, each parent will enroll their joint child(ren) in health insurance if it is offered through their employer at a reasonable cost. The parents will work together to ensure the children have the most comprehensive coverage available to them. Each parent will pay 50% of the children's uninsured medical, dental, optical, orthodontic, and mental health expenses. (Some states require that the primary or custodial parent pay the first $100-$200 and that you split any uninsured expense after that.)

5. Support.

   a. Child Support.

      i. Husband/Wife will pay to Wife/Husband, and Wife/Husband will have a judgment against Husband/Wife for the sum of $_____ per month as child support. Child support is payable on the first day of each month. Support will be paid to _____ (the state agency that collects child support). Support will be paid by wage withholding.

      ii. As additional support, each parent will provide health insurance for the minor children as long as it is available through their employment at a reasonable cost. The parents will cooperate to ensure that the children have to most comprehensive insurance possible. Each parent will provide complete information and copies of all insurance cards and any forms necessary to access the child's health insurance. Each parent is responsible for one-half of all uninsured expenses, including medical, dental, orthodontic, optical, mental health, prescriptions, and co-pays incurred on behalf of the children. Insurance payments will be directed to the provider and not to either spouse. Any overpayments will be refunded to the parent responsible for the overpayment. Both parties will use in-plan providers to the full extent possible.

   iii. Until the paying spouse's child, support obligation ends, the paying spouse will maintain a life insurance benefit in the sum of $_____ and name the minor children as the irrevocable beneficiary, in trust. The trustee will be _____ (the other parent) OR (other preferred person). The paying spouse will not cancel, encumber or alter the life insurance policy as long as he/she has a child support obligation. Within 30 days after the entry of this Judgment, the paying spouse will obtain the necessary insurance and will notify his/her insurance company of the limitations on cancelation or encumbrance and provide the insurer with a copy of this Judgment. The paying spouse will provide the receiving spouse with proof of insurance and proof of the notice to the insurance company of the restrictions of revocability and encumbrance. Should the policy owner change or encumber the policy in violation of this agreement, a constructive trust will be imposed on the paying spouse's estate, and the spouse receiving support will have a lien on the paying spouse's estate, superior to all other claims and equal to the amount the insurance.

  b. Spousal Support.

    i. Husband/Wife will pay to Wife/Husband, and Wife/Husband will have a judgment against Husband/Wife for the sum of $_____ per month as spousal support. Spousal support will terminate upon the death of either party. The factors considered in awarding spousal support are as follows: (these are suggestions and not an exhaustive list of possible factors)

1. The parties were married for _____ years and have _____ minor children and _____ adult children.
2. For the duration of the marriage, Petitioner/Respondent was the primary caretaker of children and the marital home.
3. Petitioner/Respondent supported Respondent/Petitioner in their career success to the detriment of their own; because of this, Respondent/Petitioner has much greater earning potential than Petitioner/Respondent. This is a disparity that cannot be made up or corrected with time.
4. Petitioner/Respondent's superior or advanced education was obtained with the assistance of Respondent/Petitioner.
5. There is a disparity in the earning potential of each spouse, and each spouse is entitled to maintain a lifestyle not over disparate to the lifestyle they enjoyed during the marriage.
6. Petitioner/Respondent is in good health while Respondent/Petitioner suffers from health conditions that make his/her return to the workforce difficult or impossible.
7. There are minor children in the home that require Petitioner/Respondent's care until they reach school age.
8. The parties have a disabled child that requires Petitioner/Respondent's care.

ii. Spousal support is payable on the first day of each month. Support will be paid to _____ (the state agency that collects child support). Support will be paid by wage withholding. OR Husband/Wife will deposit Wife/Husband's support into a bank account established for that purpose no later than the third day of each month.

(The date can be set to coincide with the paying spouse's pay date.)

iii. Until the paying spouse's spousal support obligation ends, the paying spouse will maintain a life insurance benefit in the sum of $_____ and name the receiving spouse as the irrevocable beneficiary. The paying spouse will not cancel, encumber or alter the life insurance policy as long as he/she has a spousal support obligation. Within 30 days after the entry of this Judgment, the paying spouse will obtain the necessary insurance and notify his/her insurance company of the limitations on cancelation or encumbrance and provide the insurer with a copy of this Judgment. The paying spouse will provide the receiving spouse with proof of insurance and proof of the notice to the insurance company of the restrictions of revocability and encumbrance. Should the policy owner change or encumber the policy in violation of this agreement, a constructive trust will be imposed on the paying spouse's estate, and the spouse receiving support will have a lien on the paying spouse's estate, superior to all other claims and equal to the amount the insurance.

iv. As additional spousal support, Petitioner/Respondent will pay, indemnify and hold Respondent/Petitioner harmless from the following marital debt:

1. _____
2. _____

6. Property.
   a. Real Property.
      i. Husband/Wife is awarded the real property located at: _____ and further identified as _____ (legal description from the property title) _____. Husband/Wife will receive the property free of any claim or encumbrance by Wife/Husband (except _____). Wife/Husband is awarded an equalizing judgment in the sum of $_____, which represents one half of the net equity in the real property. Husband/Wife must refinance the property within 90 days of the date

this Judgment is signed and remove Wife/Husband from the mortgage and satisfy the Judgment. If Husband/Wife is unable to obtain financing within 90 days of the date of this Judgment, the property will be placed for sale pursuant to Paragraph iii.

ii. OR Husband and Wife will retain the joint ownership of the real property located at: _____ and further identified as _____ (legal description from the property title) ____ as tenants in common. Wife/Husband will have exclusive use of the property until _____. Wife/Husband will pay all mortgages, encumbrances, liens, insurance, and homeowners dues payments and taxes and maintain the home in a safe and saleable condition. Upon the future sale of the property, the net equity will be split equally between the parties. The court retains jurisdiction over the parties and the real property until the sale is complete.

iii. OR The marital property will be immediately placed for sale. The court retains jurisdiction over the parties and the real property until the sale is complete. The parties will mutually agree upon a realtor and enter into a listing agreement within 14 days of the date of this Judgment. If the parties cannot agree on a realtor, each party will present a list of three possible candidates to the court, and the court will select one. If the parties cannot agree on a listing price, the judge will determine the price. The parties have a duty to deal fairly with each other and will use their best efforts to reach an agreement on the sales price, price reductions, and any other agreement surrounding the sale. The parties will share equally in the net proceeds from the sale after all mortgages and encumbrances are paid, OR the parties will divide the net proceeds as follows: (the specifics of the division should be listed here if the proceeds are not being divided equally).

b. Personal property.
    i. The Petitioner will be awarded the following personal property

1. All bank accounts in his/her individual name.
2. The (year) (make) (model) automobile (include any property with a title, such as motorcycles, boats, RVs jet-skis, snowmobiles, trailers in this section). The Petitioner will pay, indemnify and hold the Respondent harmless from the purchase money loan owing on any of the listed property. The Petitioner will have 12 months to remove Respondent's name from the purchase money loans on all property awarded to him. If Petitioner is unable to accomplish removing Respondent's name from the loan, he/she will immediately place the property for sale and apply the sale proceeds to the loan.
3. List any specific collectible or important personal property here.
4. The parties have reached an agreement, OR the court has ordered that the parties' personal property be divided pursuant to the inventory attached here as Exhibit #__.
5. All personal records and documents including but not limited to birth and adoption certificates, baptism certificates, passports, wills, military records, and record of discharge. The children's primary custodian will have custody of the children's important documents. The noncustodial parent is entitled to copies of all documents. If the noncustodial parent intends to travel with the children and requires the children's passports, the passports will be freely shared for travel and returned to the custodial parent with the child when the child returns from their travel. Neither parent will withhold the children's identity documents or other important records from the other.
6. Any claim to current or future litigation arising out of any incident that occurred during the marriage. OR The parties are the Plaintiffs in a lawsuit (describe the suit and identity it with a court case number if there is one). The parties will divide equally any proceeds

resulting from the litigation and will share equally any attorney fees and costs associated with the litigation.

c. Retirement Accounts and Investment Funds.

  i. Petitioner is awarded the entirety of the following accounts in his name: 1. ___. OR

  ii. Petitioner and Respondent will share equally in the _____ (name) fund, OR Petitioner will receive ____ (dollar amount or percentage) of the _____ (name) fund, and Respondent will receive ____ (dollar amount or percentage) of the fund. Petitioner/Respondent will retain _____ (attorney name) within 30 days of the date of this Judgment to draft and file a Qualified Domestic Relations Order (QDRO) to effect the above division. The court retains jurisdiction over the parties and their retirement funds until the division is complete.

  iii. If either party liquidates a retirement fund awarded to them, they will be solely responsible for paying any associated fees, penalties, or taxes associated with the liquidation.

d. Debts and Encumbrances.

  i. Petitioner will be responsible for all debts in his/her individual name, including all debt incurred since the parties separated on _____ (date).

  ii. The Petitioner will be responsible for paying, indemnify and hold Respondent harmless from the following joint debts, which are being paid in lieu of spousal support. 1. _____ 2. _____

  iii. Respondent will be responsible for all debts in his/her individual name, including all debt incurred since the parties separated on _____ (date).

  iv. The Respondent will be responsible for paying, indemnify and hold Respondent harmless from the following joint debts, which are being paid in lieu of spousal support. 1. _____ 2. _____

  v. Neither party will charge on the credit of the other without written permission. If either party fails to pay a joint debt as set forth in this Judgment, the other party will have the right but not the obligation to make any payment and demand reimbursement from the responsible party. Whenever the terms require one party of this Judgment to pay a joint debt, it will be deemed to be a support obligation under the Federal Bankruptcy Code, which is not dischargeable in bankruptcy as to the other party.

e. Taxes

i. The parties will file all taxes for the tax year _____ jointly. The parties will cooperate and provide all necessary documents to meet all tax filing deadlines. The parties will share equally any income tax refunds and be equally responsible for any payable taxes as a result of the joint filing.

ii. In subsequent tax years, the parties will file separate tax filings. The custodial parent will receive the deductions for all children. However, the noncustodial parent may purchase the custodial parent's deduction if to do so would benefit him/her. To accomplish this, the custodial parent will calculate her taxes with and without the child deductions. The noncustodial parent will pay the difference to the custodial parent and claim the children on his/her taxes instead. The custodial parent will execute any documents required to effect this agreement.

f. Attorney Fees. Each party will pay their own attorney fees, and court costs OR Petitioner/Respondent will pay $_____ for Respondent/Petitioner's attorney fees. Petitioner/Respondent will have a judgment against Respondent/Petitioner until such fees are paid.

g. Each party will, within 30 days, execute and deliver any and all documents required to execute the terms of this Judgment. This General Judgement will operate to convey title should either party fail to execute the necessary documents to effect the terms of this Judgment. Failure to effect the terms of this Judgment is enforceable by contempt. If either party fails to comply with the terms of this Judgment and further court proceedings are required to enforce the terms of this

Judgment, the prevailing party will recover from the other party his/her reasonable attorney fee and costs of both trial and appellate proceedings.

h. This Judgment is intended to be a full, binding, and complete resolution of the parties' divorce. Each party is hereby released from any and all claims or demands they may have against one another relating to their marriage.

i. (If the Judgment is the result of a negotiated settlement) Each party has had the opportunity to consult with independent counsel, and the entry into this Judgment is being made voluntarily and without undue influence, fraud, coercion, or misrepresentation. The parties warrant that they have made full disclosure of all assets and liabilities and that all assets and liabilities have been identified and distributed by this Judgment.

This sample judgment is by no means exhaustive of every issue because every divorce and every state are different. This sample is intended to spark discussion with your legal advisor and should not be used as a template for submission to a court.

IN THE CIRCUIT COURT OF THE STATE OF _____
    FOR THE COUNTY OF _____
        Family Court Division

Petitioner _____	)	Case Number _____
	)	PARENTING PLAN (Exhibit 1)
	)	
and	)	
Respondent _____	)	Proposed by: ☐ Petitioner
☐ Co-Petitioner	)	☐ Respondent
	)	
	)	☐ Agreed upon by both parents
	)	☐ Ordered by the Court

IMPORTANT NOTICE: The terms of your Parenting Plan will affect your legal rights and responsibilities. You should consult an attorney or your caseworker before filing your Parenting Plan with the court.

1. GOALS FOR OUR CHILDREN

This plan is intended to ensure the children's optimal development by providing continuity, stability and predictability for the children, while ensuring frequent and continued contact with each parent. Because a written plan cannot address every possible situation that might occur, the parents will implement this plan in a spirit of good faith and mutual cooperation. Parents are encouraged to re-evaluate this plan from time to time as their children's needs change.

2. WHO OUR CHILDREN ARE (additional names are listed on an attached page)

Full name	Date of Birth	Current Age	Sex (check one)
			☐ M / ☐ F
			☐ M / ☐ F
			☐ M / ☐ F
			☐ M / ☐ F

3. WHAT THE WEEKLY SCHEDULE WILL BE

> **IMPORTANT: Your decisions about how much time your children will spend in the care of each parent will have important financial implications. This decision can affect how much child support a parent is responsible for, whether a parent can claim a tax dependency deduction, etc.**

The parents acknowledge that they remain the children's parents at all times. Each parent is responsible for providing the children with a quality experience and for acting in the children's best interests.

3.1 For the purposes of describing the parenting time schedule, "**Parent A**" is the parent who the children stay with more than half the time, and "**Parent B**" is the parent who the children stay with less than half the time. If the parenting time is exactly even, it does not matter who is assigned which letter. In this document:

Parent A is (name) _____.
Parent B is (name) _____.

3.2 Weekday and Weekend Schedule:
    We will follow the schedule set forth below:

A. Parent A shall be responsible for the children's care: **(CHECK ONE)**

☐ Whenever the children are not scheduled to be with Parent B.

☐ On the following days and times:

WEEKENDS: ☐ every   ☐ every other   ☐ other

(specify) _____ from (day) _____ at __:__ _.m.

to (day) _____ at __:__ _.m.

WEEKDAYS: Specify day(s): _____ from __:__ _.m. to __:__ _.m.

OTHER (specify): _____

B. Parent B shall be responsible for the children's care on the following days and times:

WEEKENDS: ☐ every   ☐ every other   ☐ other

(specify) _____ from (day) _____ at __:__ _.m.

to (day) _____ at __:__ _.m.

WEEKDAYS: Specify day(s): _____ from __:__ _.m. to __:__ _.m.

OTHER (specify): _____

☐ There is a different parenting time schedule for the following children in Attachment 3.2(C):

(name) _____ (name) _____

(name) _____

☐ There will be a different parenting time schedule when the children reach a certain age, and it is described in Attachment 3.2 (C).

4. WHAT THE VACATION AND HOLIDAY SCHEDULE WILL BE

4.1 Summer Schedule (CHECK ONE):

☐ We will follow our weekday and weekend schedule during the summer. (SKIP TO 4.2)

☐ We will follow our weekday and weekend schedule during the summer, except that each parent shall have the opportunity to spend weeks of uninterrupted vacation time with the children each summer. We will confirm our vacation schedules in writing by the end of each year. (SKIP TO 4.2)

☐ We will follow a different parenting time schedule during the summer:
  ☐ Parent A shall be responsible for the children's care At
  ☐ all times not specified in B below.
  ☐ On the following days and times:
WEEKENDS: ☐ every ☐ every other ☐ other (specify)
_____ from (day) _____ at __:__ _.m. to (day)
_____ at __:__ _.m.
WEEKDAYS: Specify day(s): _____ from __:__ _.m. to __:__ _.m.
OTHER (specify): _____
    Parent B shall be responsible for the children's care on the following days and times:
WEEKENDS: ☐ every ☐ every other ☐ other (specify)
_____ from (day) _____ at __:__ _.m. to (day)
_____ at __:__ _.m.
WEEKDAYS: Specify day(s): _____ from __:__ _.m. to __:__ _.m.
OTHER (specify): _____

4.2 School Breaks and Holiday Schedule (CHECK ONE):

☐ We will follow our weekday and weekend schedule for all holidays and school breaks. If we choose to vary from the regular schedule for a holiday or break, we will follow the rules for temporary schedule changes in paragraph 4.4 below. (SKIP TO 4.3)

☐ We will follow the Detailed Holiday Schedule below for any holiday or school break selected. If we want to make special plans for a specific holiday, we have placed a check mark (✓) next to that holiday. For the holidays we check, this schedule overrides the weekday and weekend schedule above. If we haven't checked a holiday, we will follow the weekday and weekend schedule above.

DETAILED HOLIDAY SCHEDULE

CHECK ONLY ONE BOX IN EACH COLUMN/ CHECK ONLY ONE BOX IN EACH COLUMN

✓	HOLIDAY	Parent A:_____ (same parent's name as in paragraph 3.1)	Parent B:_____ (same parent's name as in paragraph 3.1)
☐	Spring Break	Begin day and time:_____ End day and time: _____ Every Year Odd Years Even Years **(For School Aged Children)** First half of the school Spring Break. Other Plan: _____	Begin day and time:_____ End day and time: _____ Every Year Odd Years Even Years **(For School Aged Children)** Second half of the school Spring Break.
☐	Mother's Day	Our children shall spend the day with Mother every Mother's Day from 9 a.m. until 6 p.m. Other Plan: _____	
☐	Memorial Day / Weekend	Begin day and time:_____ End day and time: _____ Every Year Odd Years Even Years Other Plan: _____	Begin day and time:_____ End day and time: _____ Every Year Odd Years Even Years
☐	Father's Day	Our children shall spend the day with Father every Father's Day from 9 a.m. until 6 p.m. Other Plan: _____	

✓	HOLIDAY	Parent A:_____	Parent B:_____
		(same parent's name as in paragraph 3.1)	(same parent's name as in paragraph 3.1)
☐	Fourth of July	Begin day and time:_____ End day and time: _____ Every Year Odd Years Even Years ☐ Other Plan: _____	Begin day and time:_____ End day and time: _____ Every Year Odd Years Even Years
☐	Labor Day / Weekend	Begin day and time:_____ End day and time: _____ Every Year Odd Years Even Years ☐ Other Plan: _____	Begin day and time:_____ End day and time: _____ Every Year Odd Years Even Years
☐	Thanksgiving Day/ Thanksgiving Break	Begin day and time:_____ End day and time: _____ Every Year Odd Years Even Years ☐ **Age Specific Plan.** If our children are in different age groups, we will follow the plan for the ☐ **youngest** child ☐ **oldest** child. **For children under age 3**: From 9 a.m. until 6 p.m. on Thanksgiving Day in even years. **For children age 3 and older**: From 6 p.m. on Wednesday evening prior to Thanksgiving until 6 p.m. on the Sunday following Thanksgiving in even years. ☐ Other Plan:	Begin day and time:_____ End day and time: _____ Every Year Odd Years Even Years ☐ **Age Specific Plan.** If our children are in different age groups, we will follow the plan for the ☐ **youngest** child ☐ **oldest** child. **For children under age 3**: From 9 a.m. until 6 p.m. on Thanksgiving Day in odd years. **For children age 3 and older**: From 6 p.m. on Wednesday evening prior to Thanksgiving until 6 p.m. on the Sunday following Thanksgiving in odd years.

✓	HOLIDAY	Parent A:_____	Parent B:_____
		(same parent's name as in paragraph 3.1)	(same parent's name as in paragraph 3.1)

☐ **Christmas/ Winter Break**

Parent A	Parent B
Begin day and time:_____	Begin day and time:_____
End day and time: _____	End day and time: _____
Every Year Odd Years Even Years	Every Year Odd Years Even Years

Parent A column:

☐ **Age Specific Plan.** If our children are in different age groups, we will follow the plan for the ☐ **youngest** child ☐ **oldest** child.

For children under age 1: From 9 a.m. until 6 p.m. on Dec. 24th in odd years and from 9 a.m. until 6 p.m. on Dec. 25th in even years.

For children between 12 months and 36 months: From 6 p.m. on Dec. 24th. until 6 p.m. on Dec. 25th in odd years and from 6 p.m. on Dec. 25th. until 6 p.m. on Dec. 26th in even years.

For children age 3 and older: From noon on the day after school ends until noon on Dec. 26th in odd years and from noon on Dec 26th until noon on the day before school resumes in even years.

☐ Other Plan:
_____
_____
_____
_____

Parent B column:

☐ **Age Specific Plan.** If our children are in different age groups, we will follow the plan for the **youngest** child **oldest** child.

For children under age 1: From 9 a.m. until 6 p.m. on Dec. 24th in even years and from 9 a.m. until 6 p.m. on Dec. 25th in odd years.

For children between 12 months and 36 months: From 6 p.m. on Dec. 24th. until 6 p.m. on Dec. 25th in even years. From 6 p.m. on Dec. 25th. until 6 p.m. on Dec. 26th in odd years.

For children age 3 and older: From noon on the day after school ends until noon on Dec. 26th in even years and from noon on Dec 26th until noon on the day before school resumes in odd years.

☐ **New Year's Eve/New Year's Day**

(odd/even is based on New Year's Day)

Parent A	Parent B
Begin day and time:_____	Begin day and time:_____
End day and time: _____	End day and time: _____
Every Year Odd Years Even Years	Every Year Odd Years Even Years
☐ Other Plan: _____	☐ Other Plan: _____

☐ **Children's birthdays**

Parent A	Parent B
Begin day and time:_____	Begin day and time:_____
End day and time: _____	End day and time: _____
Every Year Odd Years Even Years	Every Year Odd Years Even Years
☐ Other Plan: _____	☐ Other Plan: _____

☐ All three-day weekends not listed above	(Federal holidays, school in service days, etc.) ☐ If a parent has our children on a weekend with an unspecified holiday or non-school day attached, the children shall be in that parent's care for the holiday or non-school day. ☐ Other Plan: _____	
☐ Other holiday or day of significance to the family: _____	Begin day and time:_____ End day and time: _____ Every Year Odd Years Even Years ☐ Other Plan: _____	Begin day and time:_____ End day and time: _____ Every Year Odd Years Even Years
☐ Other holiday or day of significance to the family: _____	Begin day and time:_____ End day and time: _____ Every Year Odd Years Even Years ☐ Other Plan: _____	Begin day and time:_____ End day and time: _____ Every Year Odd Years Even Years

4.3 Primary Residence (CHECK ONE):

☐ Parent A's home shall be considered the "primary residence."

☐ Neither parent's home shall be considered the "primary residence."

4.4 Temporary Changes to Parenting Time. Temporary changes to the parenting time schedule may be made at any time if both parents agree ahead of time. **(CHECK ONE)**

☐ The parents **may agree verbally** to any temporary changes in the parenting time schedule.

☐ The parents **must agree on** temporary changes to the parenting time schedule **in writing**.

5. HOW WE WILL EXCHANGE OUR CHILDREN

5.1 Timeliness. Parents will arrive within minutes of the time they are scheduled to be with the children. If an unavoidable delay occurs, the delayed parent shall contact the other parent immediately.

5.2 Exchange Point/Transportation. Unless otherwise agreed by the parties, exchange of the children will be: **(CHECK ONE)**

☐ The home of the parent who is beginning his or her time with the children. The parent who is ending their time with the children shall be responsible for dropping them off at the other parent's home.

Drop off at Parent A's home shall be at the ☐ front door ☐ curbside ☐ other:_____.

Drop off at Parent B's home shall be at the ☐ front door ☐ curbside ☐ other:_____.

☐ A neutral place as follows: _____.

The parents shall share responsibility for bringing the children to and from the exchange point.

☐ Other: _____.

Additional provisions: **(OPTIONAL—CHECK ALL THAT APPLY)**
☐ If a parent starts his or her parenting time while the children are at school or in daycare, that parent shall pick the children up directly at the school or daycare. If the children are supposed to be at school or in daycare at the end of a parent's scheduled parenting time, that parent shall drop the children off directly at the school or daycare.

☐ If either parent is unable to provide transportation on a given occasion, he or she may designate one of the following individuals to do so: _____. These individuals are known to the children.

☐ Other: _____.

5.3 Clothing & Medication. The parents shall have the children ready with the clothing they need and any necessary medications at the scheduled time of exchange. All clothing and medications that accompanied the children shall be returned with them to the other parent.

5. HOW WE WILL MAKE DECISIONS ABOUT OUR CHILDREN

> **IMPORTANT NOTICE: Your decision to select Joint or Sole Custody may have important legal consequences. You are strongly encouraged to consult with an attorney regarding these consequences before making your final decision about Joint or Sole Custody.**

6.1 Day-to-Day Decisions. Each parent will make day-to-day decisions regarding the care and control of our children during the time they are caring for our children. This includes any emergency decisions affecting the health or safety of our children.

6.2 Major Decisions (Legal Custody). Major decisions include, but are not limited to, decisions about the children's residence, education, non-emergency health care, and religious training. **(CHECK ONE)**

☐ The parents have agreed to share in the responsibility for making major decisions about the children. This arrangement is known by the courts as **Joint Custody.**

☐ _____ (parent's name) shall make major decisions about the children. This arrangement is known by the courts as **Sole Custody.**

(OPTIONAL)
☐ The custodial parent will consult (discuss) with the other parent:
   ☐ before making major decisions
   ☐ before making major decisions on these specific issues:

_____.

(OPTIONAL)
The custodial parent will notify the other parent:
   ☐ before making major decisions
   ☐ before making major decisions on these specific issues:

_____.

Note: If this parenting plan is attached to a signed order or judgment of the court, the custody provisions in the plan should be consistent with what is in the judgment or order. In the event of a conflict, the custody designation in the signed order or judgment shall prevail.

6.3 Information Sharing. Unless there is a court order stating otherwise:

Both parents have equal rights to inspect and receive the children's school records, and both parents are encouraged to consult with school staff concerning the children's welfare and education.

Both parents are encouraged to participate in and attend the children's school events.

Both parents have equal rights to inspect and receive governmental agency and law enforcement records concerning the children.

Both parents have equal rights to consult with any person who may provide care or treatment for the children and to inspect and receive the children's medical, dental, and psychological records.

Each parent has a continuing responsibility to provide a residential, mailing, or contact address and contact telephone number to the other parent.

Each parent has a continuing responsibility to immediately notify the other parent of any emergency circumstances or substantial changes in the health of the children, including the children's medical needs.

7. HOW WE WILL COMMUNICATE ABOUT AND WITH OUR CHILDREN

7.1 Parent and Child Communication.
☐ Both parents and children shall have the right to communicate by telephone, in writing or by e-mailing during reasonable hours without interference or monitoring by the other parent.
☐ Rules for telephone, letters, e-mail or other parent and child communication: (DESCRIBE) _____
_____.

7.2 Parent to Parent Communication.
☐ Rules for telephone, letters, e-mail or other parent-to-parent communication: (DESCRIBE) _____
_____.

8. FUTURE MOVES BY A PARENT. Unless there is a court order stating otherwise neither parent may move to a residence more than 60 miles further away from the other parent without giving the other parent _____ days' notice of the change of residence and providing a copy of such notice to the court.
Additional rules about moving: (DESCRIBE) _____
_____.

9. OTHER PROVISIONS ON HOW WE WILL WORK TOGETHER FOR OUR CHILDREN

9.1 Children's Activities. Children are often involved in activities other than school, such as sports, clubs, music, religious organizations, and social activities. Both parents are encouraged to take part in non-school activities with their children during their parenting time. Non-school activities should not unreasonably interfere with either parent's schedule and parenting time. Non-school activities that may affect the other parent's schedule: **(CHECK ONE)**
   ☐ Must be coordinated with the other parent.
   ☐ Will be planned to occur primarily during one parent's scheduled parenting time.
   ☐ Other:_____.

9.2 Makeup and Missed Parenting Time.
If a child is so ill that the child is unable to spend time with a parent, there will be no make-up of parenting time unless the parents agree: **(CHECK ONE)**
   ☐ in writing
   ☐ verbally
If a parent is unable to have the children during his or her scheduled parenting time for any reason, there will be no make-up of parenting time unless the parents agree: **(CHECK ONE)**

☐ in writing
☐ verbally

9.3 Mutual Respect. The parents will not say things or knowingly allow others to say things in the presence of the children that would take away the children's love and respect for the other parent.

9.4 Alternate Care. These are our ground rules for babysitters, day care providers, and other caregivers: **(CHECK ALL THAT APPLY)**
☐ We choose not to specify ground rules for alternate care.

☐ If a parent is unable to be with the children during scheduled parenting time, the other parent shall be the first choice to provide of their care.

☐ Only the following people may provide alternate care: _____.

☐ The following people may not provide alternate care: _____.

☐ Other: _____
_____.

9.5 Other Items. **(ADD ANY OTHER ITEMS YOU WOULD LIKE TO INCLUDE IN YOUR PLAN)**
☐ 9.5 (a)
☐ Additional page attached (Attachment 9.5).

10. PERMANENT CHANGES TO THE SCHEDULE. Permanent changes can be made only by applying to the court for a modification. One parent cannot change a court-ordered Parenting Plan on their own.

11. DISPUTE RESOLUTION. We will try to work out any parenting plan disputes on our own. Only as a last resort will we resolve disputes through court action. (Local court rules will apply after filing a court action) Prior to filing any court action: **(CHECK ONE)**
☐ We will use a mutually agreed-upon, neutral third-party (such as a mediator, counselor, or other professional) to resolve any parenting

plan disputes before filing a court action about the parenting plan. This shall not apply in the event of an emergency or abusive circumstance. (OPTIONAL) For now, the following professional(s) will assist us, if available:

_____

_____.

☐ A dispute resolution process shall not be required prior to filing a court action.

12. SIGNATURES. My signature below indicates that I have read and agree with what has been decided and written in this document.

☐ Petitioner   ☐ Respondent

_____   _____

Signature   Date   Signature   Date

NOTES

CHAPTER 3

1. "Statistics," National Coalition against Domestic Violence, accessed July 22, 2021, https://ncadv.org/STATISTICS.
2. Charles Spurgeon, "All of Grace" (sermon, Metropolitan Tabernacle, Newington, UK, published October 7, 1915), Spurgeon Archive, accessed July 22, 2021, https://archive.spurgeon.org/sermons/3479.php.
3. Brené Brown, "The Power of Vulnerability," YouTube, January 3, 2011, https://www.youtube.com/watch?v=iCvmsMzlF7o.
4. Dr. Dan Siegel, "Hand Model of the Brain," YouTube, August 9, 2017, https://www.youtube.com/watch?v=f-m2YcdMdFw.

CHAPTER 9

1. *Troxel v. Granville*, 530 US 57 (2000).

CHAPTER 10

1. Glennon Doyle, Untamed (New York: Dial, 2020), 142.
2. "Child Sexual Abuse Statistics," Darkness to Light, accessed July 22, 2021, https://www.d2l.org/wp-content/uploads/2017/01/all_statistics_20150619.pdf.

CHAPTER 11

1. "2020 Alzheimer's Disease Facts and Figures," Alzheimer's Association, March 10, 2020, https://alz-journals.onlinelibrary.wiley.com/doi/full/10.1002/alz.12068.

CHAPTER 12

1. *Roe v. Wade*, 410 U.S. 113 (1973).

CHAPTER 13

1. "Female Troops and Their Shocking Divorce Rate," Military.com, March 15, 2015, https://www.military.com/spousebuzz/blog/2015/03/female-troops-and-their-shocking-divorce-rate.html.
2. "VA National Suicide Data Report 2005–2016," Office of Mental Health and Suicide Prevention, September 2018, https://www.mentalhealth.va.gov/docs/data-sheets/OMHSP_National_Suicide_Data_Report_2005-2016_508.pdf.
3. "Department of Defense Annual Report on Sexual Assault in the Military: Fiscal Year 2018," Marines, May 2, 2019, https://www.marines.mil/News/Press-Releases/Press-Release-Display/Article/1833817/department-of-defense-fiscal-year-2018-annual-report-on-sexual-assault-in-the-m/.

CHAPTER 23

1. Theodore Roosevelt, "Citizenship in a Republic" (speech given at the Sorbonne, Paris, France, April 23, 1910).

INDEX

ABOUT THE AUTHOR

Lori Hellis has been a family and criminal defense lawyer since 1992. It's safe to say she's seen it all. Lori has represented hundreds of divorce clients during some of the most challenging times in their lives. She knows that maintaining equilibrium and a sense of humor is crucial when navigating the minefields of divorce.

Lori holds a bachelor of arts degree in journalism from the University of Portland in Portland, Oregon, where she graduated Magna Cum Laude. She has a doctor of law degree from Lewis and Clark Northwestern School of Law in Portland, Oregon, and a master of fine arts degree in creative writing from Oregon State University. She recently retired from law practice to devote time to writing.

Lori was also a fierce public defender who represented both adults and juveniles in criminal matters. She served twenty years in the U.S. Air National Guard and has been a passionate advocate for children, victims of domestic violence, and veterans.

Lori lives in Mesa, Arizona, with her husband, two dogs, and three cats. She is a podcast junkie and a maker of quilts. She has one adult daughter who has always seemed proud that her mother wore combat boots.